The first known Winchester Repeating Arms Company catalog appeared in 1867. Illustrated Appendix A lists and describes over 300 pieces of promotional printed material published from the first to 1983.

WINCHESTER
SHOTGUNS AND SHOTSHELLS

Ronald W. Stadt

1984

ARMORY PUBLICATIONS: TACOMA

to Lorraine
without whom there would have been no collecting.

Printed in the United States of America by
Braun-Brumfield, Incorporated
100 North Staebler Road
Ann Arbor, Michigan 48106

Library of Congress Catalog Card Number: 83-073409

ISBN-0-9604982-2-2

First Edition

ACKNOWLEDGEMENTS

I have been encouraged by many collectors and friends to pursue this "fun" work. Lewis Yearout published my first Winchester article and Mike Stuckslager continued to present what are now chapters in *The Winchester Collector*. George Madis has been an idol and a supplier of specific information. Grant Tom, John Dyer, Michael McIntosh, Ron Willis, Homer E. Clark Jr., and other gun lovers gave freely of their memory of Winchester guns. James C. Tillinghast and Ron Willis contributed immensely to the appendix on printed material. Felix A. Bedlan shared all that he knew about ventilated ribs on Model 12's. Ernie Simmons Jr. recalled all that he could on the same subject. Jim Stotts and other Olin employees including Mike Evernham and Paul Meyers did all they could to ensure that I was on the right track. Joyce Berrman gave suggestions about the poems and insisted that the book go first class. Laura Mauch offered improvements for which only a lay person could see need. Whimp Ewell, Buddy Caldbeck and other shotshell collectors showed more than courteous interest in a related field. George Hoyem was at once encouraging, later constructive re addition of information regarding shotshells and boxes, and finally insistent upon high quality.

CONTENTS

INTRODUCTION

Winchester Shotguns and Shotshells was written for several reasons: (1) It was a labor of love. After three decades of study, Winchester guns are evermore fascinating. (2) It seemed to be needed because information concerning many of the models is quite limited and because much of what has been written about the popular models is partly in error. (3) It was an obligation. The collecting and shooting fraternities deserve a ready reference to the most diverse line of shotguns produced by an American company. And (4) it seemed appropriate to produce a book which emphasizes Winchester shotguns—there being so many which emphasize only rifles.

I attempted to explain grades in sequence for each model. I believe that understanding Winchester shotguns is best approached by becoming familiar with the grade, gauge, barrel length, choke, matting, solid or ventilated rib, wood characteristics, metal embellishment, and mechanical changes which occurred within each model. Except for the several models which were listed only in standard grade plain finished, the major organization of each chapter narrative is by grade.

The matter of grades of the early guns merits special treatment because it is the most mistreated in the literature—rivaled only by controversies about who installed which ventilated ribs. Models 1887, 1893 and 1897 were first offered in standard grade. This was sometimes called plain finished in catalogs. A number of embellishments were available on these models from their introduction. These included three- and four-blade damascus barrels, fancy grain wood, checking, rubber butt plates, and other than standard stock dimensions. Not long after introduction, these and Models 1911 and 1912 were available in Fancy Finished grade. This entailed checking, rubber butt plates and, on the Model 1887, outline or border engraving.

Models 1897, 1911, and 1912 were, much of the time, available in standard, trap and pigeon grades. The 1897's and 1912's were also made in tournament grade, which included checked wood and usually straight grips. Trap grade entailed fancy walnut and black diamonds in the grip panels. Pigeon grade required full fancy walnut, black diamonds, engraving and dimensions to order. Black diamond was never a grade designation. Trap did not mean for trap shooting only. All gauges were available in trap grade. All manner of barrel lengths and chokes were offered in trap grade. This is true of early 21's and 42's as well. Lots of trap grade 12's, 21's and 42's were bored skeet. These were called trap grade skeet guns in catalogs. On Model 12's and older models, Deluxe was never a grade designation. The Model 42 was made in Deluxe grade for a long time and the Model 21 was made in Deluxe grade for a short time.

The matter of options and special features is among the most fascinating topics. A large variety of options and special features were available for various periods of time. Thus you find guns which do not "fit" catalog pictures of the various grades and styles, such as Brush and Duck. Engraving varies a great deal and may be found on any grade or style—though likely not on riot and certainly not on trench guns. Most of the engraving variations shown in catalogs are found on Model 12's and Model 21's. However, there are many exceptions from the very early Model 1887's to World War II at least. Early catalogs which described highly finished arms did not feature shotguns. However, very elaborate examples of engraved Model 1887's, 1893's and 1897's exist. Straight and half pistol grips were available as options or at extra cost on the major models, excepting the 1887 and 1901. Damascus barrels were available on 1887's, 1893's and 1897's. Matted barrels were available on 1897's, 1911's and 1912's. Matted ribs were available on 1912's and 42's and not on the earlier models. The approach of the Winchester Repeating Arms Company was, for many years, to develop a full line of guns through careful evolution. At one time the line included lever, slide, and auto loading actions.Later it included slide, double barrel, and single shot models. Later still it included slide, auto loading, double barrel, and single shot models. Some developments were adapted to all of the models in the line at the time. Most, however, were adapted to only some models. Example—ventilated ribs were available only on the Model 12's, 21's, 42's, and 50's.

The matter of overlapping is especially fascinating. Some features were supplied in limited fashion, e.g., orders for custom work, before they became standard or catalog options. Often a grade or style, or lesser option, was available before it was given a special designation and advertised, e.g., the 20 gauge magnum Model 21, the Model 21 Custom, Pigeon, and Grand American, and the fancy finished Model 1887. In many instances, transition pieces occurred—an 1897 with an 1893 action slide, a 1901 without markings of any kind, a Model 12 TRAP with black diamonds. Many of these exist because, after changes were authorized, parts supplies were used before changes were fully implemented. Pieces with unusual combinations of features also occurred because of parts cleanup after a model was discontinued. Examples include a Model 97 solid frame with a serial number very near the end of 1897 production, an unfired 16 gauge Model 97 with a "D" serial number and wood which appeared much later on "E" guns.

It is likely that some features listed in catalogs were never produced. Model 50's with certain engraving styles have not been seen. Likewise, some features which were never listed in catalogs exist. A 16 gauge Model 12 with factory ventilated rib is a startling example.

The following chapters deal with these and other matters in careful and guarded fashion. Each begins with a catalog description and proceeds with a description of grades. Special notes sections deal with characteristics such as barrel lengths, ribs, embellishments, mechanical changes, and common failures. For all of these, dates of authorization, introduction, discontinuance and last availability are given as accurately as possible.

The pictures of shotshells and boxes and dates of introduction and discontinuance are at the center of a subject too large for this book but deserving of enough coverage to show paralleling chronologies.

The final chapter—How To Design A Collection—should help you decide long in advance which of the many models and variations you want to seek. There are far too many alternatives to permit buying any gun which comes along.

The appendices will be helpful if you should wish to acquire material which describe certain models, if you wish to collect printed material as many are now doing, or if you wish to understand the limitations of dating guns via serial numbers.

Shotguns introduced after the Model 59 are not treated because they are of little concern to collectors.

Ron Stadt

WINCHESTER!

That's the name you can't forget.
That's the name you won't regret.
It was the name on guns from 79 to 81.
And every father's son wanted one.
Chances are it was a model 12 or 24.
It could have been a 37 or many more.
It could have been a pump or a single.
It could have been an auto or a double.
It could have been a twenty gauge.
It could have been some other gauge.
It could have been a plain ole gun.
It could have been a fancy one.
No matter which it was it shot game pretty good.
No matter which it was it lasted like you knew it would.
No matter when it was new it's still around I'll bet.
No matter how old it is somebody uses it yet.
No matter what it's like it shoots real nice.
No matter what it cost it's worth the price.
After all it's a Winchester.
A gun to be respected, mister.

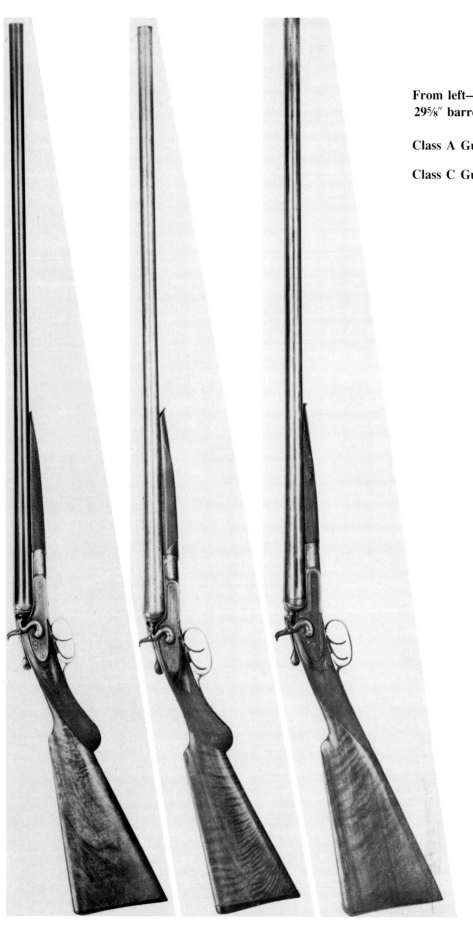

From left—Match Gun no. 1310, 16 ga., 29⅝″ barrel.

Class A Gun no. 1044, 12 ga., 30″.

Class C Gun no. 1088, 10 ga., 30″.

Chapter 1

HAMMER DOUBLES 1879–1884

The saga of Winchester shotguns began with imported guns. Barnes et al. (1980, pp. 21–22) reported that in 1878 P. G. Sanford was sent as agent of Winchester to Birmingham, England and while there was instructed to purchase cheaper grades of double barrel shotguns for shipment to its New York Sales Depot. Winchester had no facilities for making such arms. The literature reports that guns were purchased from Messrs. W. C. McAntree & Company, Richard Rodman, C. G. Bonehill, and Messrs. W. C. Scott & Sons. The Scott-made guns were probably the higher grades. The first guns were not marked. Because they sold very quickly, Winchester decided to import the better ones. A loose-leaf insert in the 1879 catalog listed five grades: Match Gun, Class A, Class B, Class C, and Class D. The 1880 Sales Depot Catalog provided details of the five grades and identified a sixth grade, the Club Gun, which was much like the Class A.

WINCHESTER REPEATING ARMS CO., "MATCH GUN":

Fine laminated steel barrels, full choke, fine steel bar rebounding locks, Scott's patent top lever, Purdy's Double Bolt, extension rib, solid head strikers, patent forearm snap, half pistol hand, low hammers, and horn buttplate. Drop of stock 2⅞ inches. Pull 14⅛. This is a very fine finished gun, (engraved nicely):

Weight of 12 bore	30 in. barrel	7¼–7¾ lbs.
Weight of 10 bore	32 in. barrel	8¼–8¾ lbs.

Price $85.00

WINCHESTER REPEATING ARMS CO., "CLASS A" GUN:

Fine laminated steel barrels, left barrel choke, fine steel bar rebounding locks, Top Lever, Purdy's double bolt, patent forearm snap, half pistol hand, and low hammers. A nice finished gun throughout:

Drop of stock, 2⅞ inch   Length of same 14⅛ inch

Weight of 12 bore	with 30 inch barrel	7¼ to 7¾ lbs.
Weight of 10 bore	with 32 inch barrel	8¼ to 8¾ lbs.

Price $70.00

WINCHESTER REPEATING ARMS CO., "CLASS B" GUN:

Laminated steel barrels, fine steel bar locks, rebounding hammers, patent top lever, double bolt, patent forearm snap, half pistol hand.

Drop of stock, 2⅞ inch   Length of same 14⅛ inch

Weight of 12 bore	with 30 inch barrel	7¼ to 7¾ lbs.
Weight of 10 bore	with 32 inch barrel	8¼ to 8¾ lbs.

Price $60.00

WINCHESTER, "CLASS C" GUN:

Laminated steel barrels, steel bar lock, rebounding hammers, patent top lever, double bolt. A fine and serviceable gun.

Drop of stock, 2⅞ inch   Length of same 14⅛ inch

Weight of 12 bore	with 30 inch barrel	7¼–7¾ lbs.
Weight of 10 bore	with 32 inch barrel	8¼–8¾ lbs.

Price $50.00

The first Winchester brass shells may have had no headstamp. The first listed were the "XX." Gauges, years introduced, and years discontinued were: 8 and 10, 1877–1881; 11, 1877–1878; 12, 1878–1881; 14, 1877–1881; 15; 1877–1878; 16, 1877–1881; 20, 1877–1881.

English craftsmen took great pains on Match Guns. Wood to metal fit and engraving on this specimen (first gun in previous illustration) are very well executed. Note the graceful hammers, the running dog, and the WRA Co with "&" on the trigger guard.

WINCHESTER, "CLASS D" GUN:

Best English twist barrels, steel bar lock, lever underguard. A good service-able gun.

Drop of stock, 2⅞ inch   Length of same 14⅛ inch
Weight of 12 bore   with 30 inch barrel   7¼–7¾ lbs.
Weight of 10 bore   with 32 inch barrel   8¼–8¾ lbs.
Price $40.00

All of these guns are furnished with fine English Walnut stocks with checked grip and forearm.

Obviously, the higher grades had more quality features, including more profuse engraving. It is not known which manufacturer made the various guns. "Winchester Repeating Arms Co. (grade) New Haven Conn. U.S.A." was engraved south to north on the top ribs. Side plates which I have examined were engraved Winchester Repeating Arms Co. Match Gun or Class A (three lines) and Winchester Class C (two lines).

Little is known about serial numbers. Some were as high as 10,000. They were probably from makers' sequences and not indicative of the number of Winchester-marked guns. All of these guns have English proof marks. Match Guns and perhaps some Class A guns had "WRA Co" engraved on the trigger guard.

Mr. Sanford made trips to England to purchase the Winchester-branded hammer doubles. They were sold only through the New York store. In 1884, Winchester decided to discontinue selling guns it did not make. According to Barnes et al. (1980, p. 22) remaining guns were sold to John P. Moore & Son on May 12, 1884. Barnes et al. indicated that approximately 10,000 were imported. On page 11 of the June 1981 *Winchester Arms Collector*, Lewis E. Yearout reported that the June 12 and June 19, 1884 editions of *Forest and Stream* contained advertisements by Edwin S. Harris, 177 Broadway, New York, New York which indicated that he had purchased the remaining stock at a job price and would sell them at less than before offered. Perhaps Harris bought them from John P. Moore and Son.

Number 1310 is exemplary of what shotgun collectors should seek to buy, i.e., the highest grade in the smallest gauge and best condition. It is a Match Gun with all of the features described above. The stock is rather fancy European walnut, checked about 18 lines per inch. The action parts are moderately covered with scroll engraving. The rear of the front-action side plates have oval vignettes with a running, long-haired (rather indistinguishable) dog on the left and two gamebirds (probably grouse) on the right. The trigger guard has the WRA Co engraving. Of all things it includes an "&" sign. The engraver must have inserted the & unwittingly. What makes this gun worth mentioning is that it has 29¹¹⁄₁₆″ *16 gauge* barrels. This is the only 16 gauge known to me. It is immaculate and a joy to its owner.

Winchester first offered empty paper shotshells in 1877. Loaded shells were not offered until 1894. The first shells (not shown) were headstamped "WRA Co." and were available from 1877 to 1879 in 10 and 12 gauge. They were brown. The next empty shells, also brown, were headstamped "WINCHESTER" (specimen above). Gauges, year introduced, and year discontinued were: 4, 1879–1884; 8, 10, 12, 14, 16 and 20, all brought out in 1878 and dropped in 1884. These were followed by a dark gray empty shell (below) made from 1883 to 1884 in 4, 8, 10, 12, 14, 16 and 20 gauge.

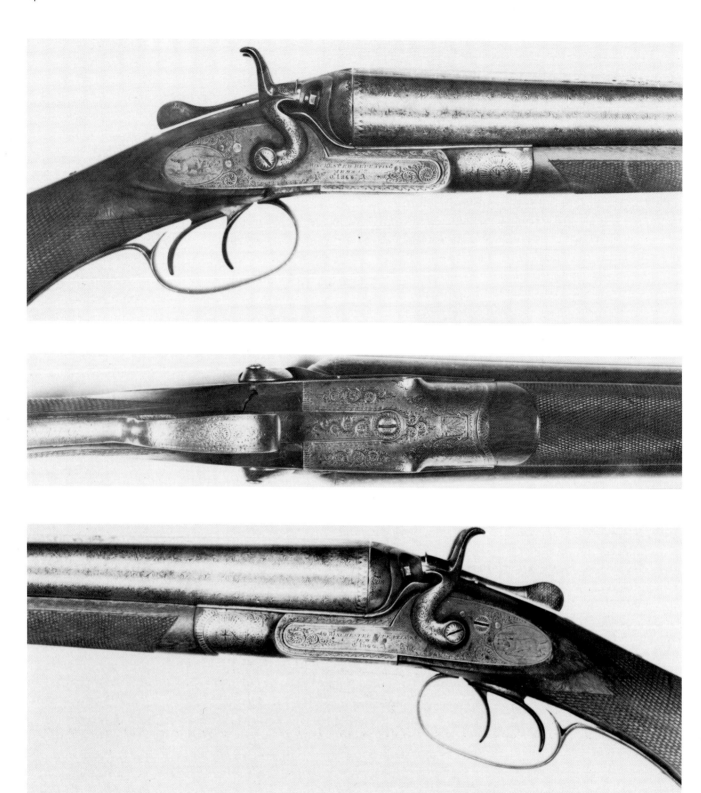

Class A guns were almost as ornate as Match Guns. The running and pointing dogs on this specimen are not quite up to the quality of that on the Match Gun.

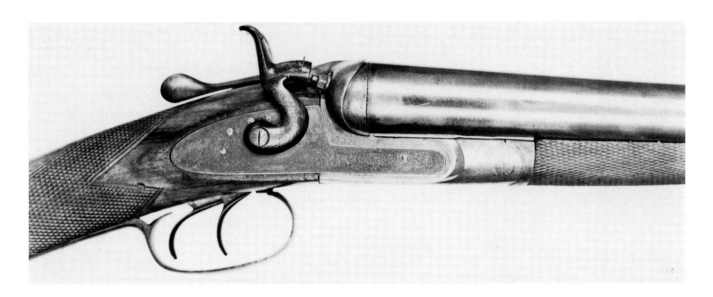

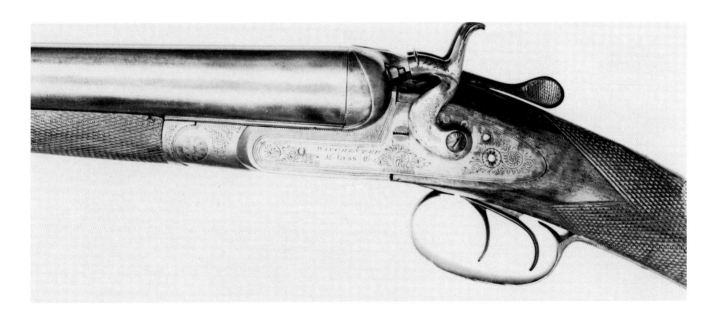

Class C guns were not nearly as ornate as the high quality grade guns. Note the wedge fastener for the forearm.

The entire line of empty paper shotshells was changed in 1884. "1st Quality" shells with the WINCHESTER headstamp (at left) were black. Gauges, year introduced and year discontinued were: 4, 1884–1897; 8, 1884–1898; 10, 12, 14, 16, 20, 1884–1894; .58 cal. unknown.

"2nd Quality" shells with the W. R. A. Co. S. Q. headstamp were offered in 10 and 12 gauge from 1884 to 1894. The 12's were black. The 10's were gray.

Star shells were offered from 1884 to 1894 in 10 and 12 gauges. They also were black. This rare Star box is cream with blue print.

The upper-right two shells are "1st Quality." Note the two sizes of letters. Gauges, year introduced, and year discontinued were: 4, 1886–1909; 8, 1878–1923; 10, 1878–1949; 12, 1878–1949; 14, 1878–1919; 16, 1878–1949; 20, 1878–1949; .410 bore, 1927–1933; .58 cal., 1881–1919. No. 3 Yacht Cannon empty brass shells were furnished but not listed.

Rival meant second quality. This headstamp replaced XX. Gauges, year introduced and year discontinued were: 10, 1884–1929; 12, 1884–1929; 28, 1914–1949.

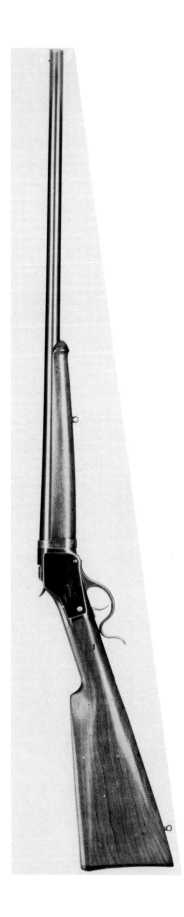

Chapter 2

1885 SINGLE SHOT

A year after introduction of the Model 12 and likely because of the popularity of the 20 gauge repeater, Winchester introduced the 1885 Single Shot Shotgun in solid frame and takedown styles. The first announcement was a November 1913 letter to the trade which described both solid and takedown frames. Two pages in the shotgun section of the 1914 catalog were devoted to the 20 gauge single shot. (Some 20 gauge high walls had been made since 1887, but formal promotion was begun in 1913.) The catalog description tells much of the story. The line about Sharp's is pure advertising license.

> The construction of the new Winchester Single Shot 20 Gauge Shotgun is the same as that of the Winchester Single Shot Rifle, having the old reliable Sharp's breech-bolt and lever. This is a very simple and strong form of construction and one that gives a light and easy action. The opening movement of the lever automatically withdraws the firing pin and draws down the bolt, leaving the breech clear. The closing movement leaves the hammer in a locked position at half cock. To fire the gun, the hammer must be brought to full cock by hand. When the gun is open, the barrel can be examined or cleaned from the breech. The take-down gun has the simplest kind of take-down device, it being only necessary to push forward the take-down lock, drop the lever and give the barrel a quarter turn, when the gun comes apart.
>
> The gun is made with 26 inch 20 gauge full choked nickel steel barrel, chambered for shells 3 inches in length and under. Its length over all is 41¾ inches, length of stock 13⁷⁄₁₆ inches, drop at comb 1⅞ inches and drop at heel 2¹¹⁄₁₆ inches. It weighs about 5½ lbs. It has a straight grip stock and forearm of plain walnut and is fitted with a rubber butt plate. The receiver is matted on top along the line of sight. Cylinder bore or modified choke barrels will be furnished instead of full choke barrels without extra charge; and interchangeable barrels, full choke, modified choke or cylinder bore will be furnished for take-down guns.
>
> Price List of Winchester Single Shot 20 Gauge Shotguns

Solid Frame, Single Shot 20 Gauge Shotgun, 26 inch Nickel Steel Barrel	$16.00
Take-Down, Single Shot 20 Gauge Shotgun, 26 inch Nickel Steel Barrel	21.00
Pistol Grip Stock of Plain Walnut	3.00
Interchangeable Nickel Steel Barrel, 26 inch, complete with Forearm	12.00
Matted Rib, or Matting Barrel	5.00

The 1916 catalog had the same copy. The 1918 and subsequent catalogs did not. Serial numbers are in the vicinity of 114,000. Madis (1980, p. 66) maintained that they range from 110,000 to 115,000. Number 114,200 is exactly like the catalog description for take-down guns with sling swivel studs.

The single shot was discontinued in 1920. Approximately 139,725 were made. It is likely that only several hundred were made in 20 gauge. Lew Yearout once examined a 28 gauge barrel section which was made up for a Winchester employee. A few had matted barrels. Matting was pressed into the barrel top with a roller prior to bluing. The barrel was mounted on a mandrel in a press and matting was accomplished in one pass of the roller—just like rolling on barrel markings. No solid ribs are known. No Winchester shotgun collection is complete without a Single Shot and this is one of the most difficult to acquire especially in very good or better condition.

The specimen at left is takedown no. 114XXX, 20 ga., 26″ full choke, factory studs for sling swivels.

Winchester Single Shot 20 Gauge Shotgun.
Solid Frame And "Take Down" Styles.

20 Gauge Solid Frame Single Shot Shotgun, $16.00.

Twenty-six Inch Nickel Steel Barrel, Straight Grip Stock and Forearm of Plain Walnut, not Checked, Rubber Butt Plate, Weight about 5½ pounds, ... $16.00

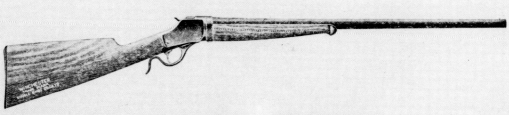

20 Gauge "Take Down" Single Shot Shotgun, $21.00.

Twenty-six Inch Nickel Steel Barrel, Straight Grip Stock and Forearm of Plain Walnut, not Checked, Rubber Butt Plate, Weight about 5¾ pounds, ... $21.00

149

S.S. Shotgun

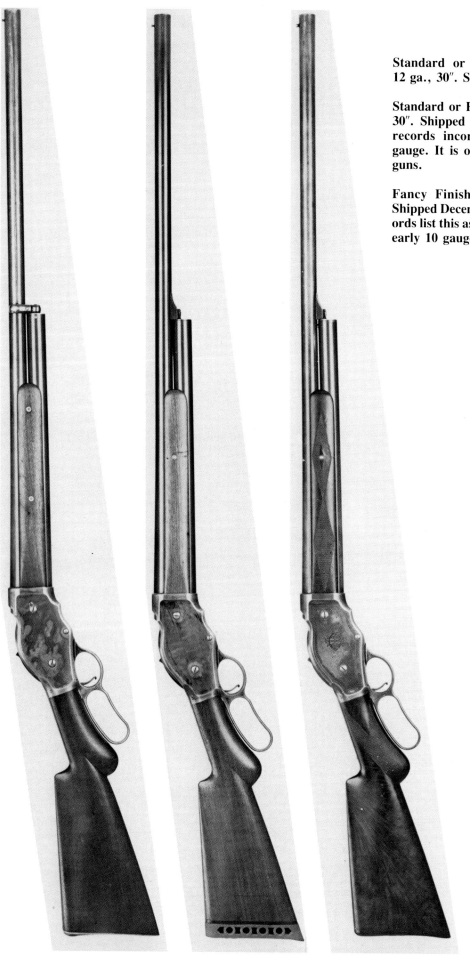

Standard or Plain Finished no. 35368, 12 ga., 30″. Shipped October 14, 1891.

Standard or Plain Finished 2217, 10 ga., 30″. Shipped August 17, 1887. Museum records incorrectly show this as a 12 gauge. It is one of the earliest 10 gauge guns.

Fancy Finished no. 6725, 10 ga., 30″. Shipped December 22, 1887. Museum records list this as a 12 gauge but it is another early 10 gauge gun. Details in text.

Chapter 3

MODELS 1887 AND 1901/01

Model 1887   1887–1901

Because Winchester's venture into the shotgun market with imported double barrels was a financial success, it considered development of a lever action shotgun which would compliment its very popular rifles. Browning Brothers' patent application was filed June 15, 1885 and U.S. Patent No. 336,287 was awarded on February 16, 1886. Winchester purchased manufacturing and sales rights in 1886 and introduced the Model 1887 in the June 1887 catalog. It was the first lever action shotgun made in the United States. The 1888 catalog had the usual glowing phrases:

> Sportsmen will find this a strong, serviceable arm. The system contains but sixteen parts in all, and can be readily understood from sectional cuts. The breech block and finger lever form one piece, and move together in opening and closing. The hammer, placed in the breech block, is automatically cocked during the closing motion; but can also be cocked or set at half-cock by hand.

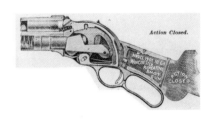

> The trigger and finger lever are so adjusted that the trigger cannot be pulled prematurely, and the gun cannot be discharged until closed. The barrel can be examined and cleaned from the breech. The magazine and carrier hold five cartridges, which with one in the chamber, make six at the command of the shooter. Anyone accustomed to shooting can readily shoot double birds with this gun.

> This gun has as yet been very little used in public. On the occasion of its first appearance, the gun divided with one other gun the first prize for fifty birds, February 22nd, 1887, at Plainfield, N.J.

> The standard gun will be made up with rolled steel barrel, case hardened frame, and pistol grip stock of plain wood, not checked. All guns will be full choked, and no gun will be sent out which will not make a good target. The standard length of barrel will be 30 or 32 inches, as may be desired. But unless otherwise ordered, guns with 30-inch barrel will in all cases be sent.

> Two kinds of Damascus barrels will be furnished when desired, at prices given below. The standard gun will have a stock 12¾ inches in length and 2⅝ inches drop; and any variation from standard length or drop will be charged for extra.

Price List (Model 1887)

Winchester Repeating Shotgun, 30 or 32 inch Barrel, 12 Gauge,	$25.00
Fancy Walnut Stock and Forearm, not checked,	$10.00
Checking Stock and Forearm,	$ 5.00
Rubber Butt Plate	$ 2.00
Good (3 blade) Damascus Barrel (additional),	$15.00
Fine (4 blade) Damascus Barrel (additional),	$20.00

According to Madis, (1981, p.102) serial number one was a fancy finished gun with Damascus barrel and checked wood, received at the warehouse on January 22 and shipped on April 16, 1887.

The February 1889 catalog contained an interesting footnote:

> About April 1st, 1889, we expect to have our 10 gauge Repeating Shotgun ready for the market. The system will be the same as the 12 gauge, with standard length of barrel 32 inches, and weight of about 9½ lbs. The list and extras will be the same as for 12 gauge.

An interesting sidelight re John M. Browning and the Model 1887 was given by Browning and Gentry (1964, pp. 111–112). Beginning on March 28, 1887, Browning spent two years as a Mormon missionary to the southern states. He first saw an 1887 in the window of a sporting goods shop in a large southern town. Despite his and his partner's unshaven, worn, and dust-covered appearance, Browning was compelled to see the gun. He went in, overwhelmed the storekeeper, opened and closed the gun several times, then threw it to his shoulder and operated it very rapidly as though shooting at flushed quail. Troubled by the disparity between Browning's appearance and expertise, the storekeeper observed that Browning knew how to handle the gun. When Browning's companion said "He ought to, he invented it," the storekeeper took the gun and put it back in the window.

Standard or Plain Finished 12 gauge 1887–1901
10 gauge 1888–1901

Early standard guns had no grade designation. The March 1898 and subsequent catalogs called them plain finished. The extras shown above continued to be listed. Thus, what is plain or fancy finished may be difficult to judge.

Riot guns were first listed in the March 1898 catalog and were made in 12 and 10 gauge with 20 inch barrels. "These guns are used by express messengers, watchmen, prison guards, train hands, and by many people for home defense. They are far superior to a revolver for shooting in the dark. . . ."

Fancy Finished 12 and 10 gauge 1898–1901

This grade designation appeared in catalogs beginning with number 61 in March 1898. It was merely a label for 1887's with certain of the extras available from the start. The fancy finished gun pictured in the catalog had checked wood, Damascus barrel, and outline engraving only on the receiver sides.

The March 1898 catalog had an extra line of type which read: "Send for our handsomely illustrated 24 page catalogue showing the engraving and checking on fancy guns." Subsequent catalogs did not have this statement. I have not examined the 24-page catalog. The October, 1897 28-page "Highly Finished Arms" catalog pictured only rifles. It mentioned the entire line of guns but one cannot discern from it whether there were standard styles of engraving for the 1887 over and above the simple outline engraving pictured in regular catalogs.

Several guns illustrate the fact that several grades of engraving were supplied on special order. Number 6725 is a 10 gauge with 30 inch four-blade Damascus barrel, outline engraving on the receiver sides, three superimposed engraved letters in a field of light scroll on the right hand side, extremely fancy checked wood, and rubber butt plate. This 10 gauge was shipped in December 1887.

Number 3462 was described by Madis (1981, p. 100). It has a four blade Damascus barrel, outline engraving on the receiver sides and shoulders, superimposed "WHT" on the right side and light scroll engraving on the receiver sides, fancy checked wood, and rubber butt plate.

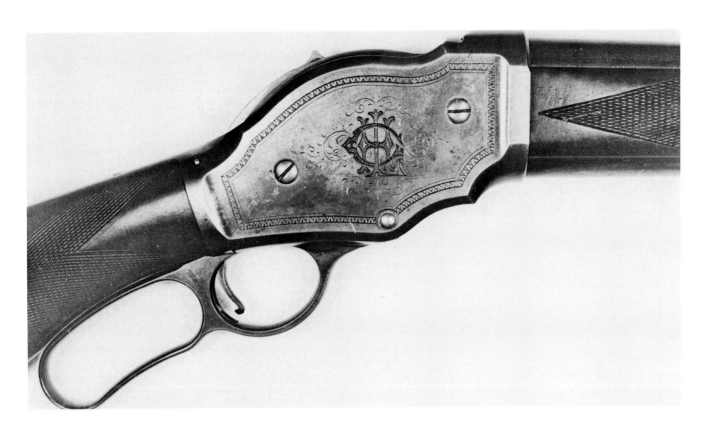

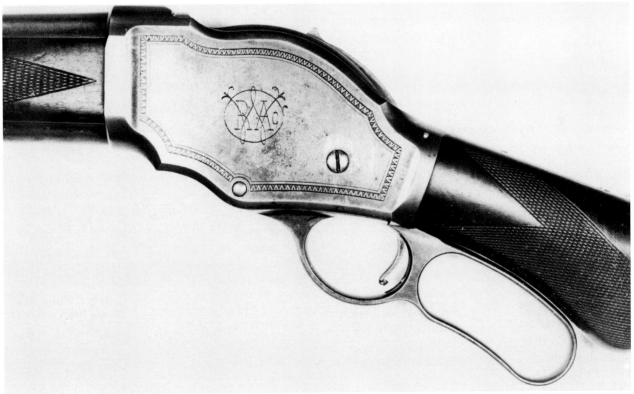

Details of the 10 ga. no 6725 shown at right on p. 10. The intertwined letters on the right side of the action are "CHL," on the left "WRA Co." On the Model 1887 action the hammer is nearly flush with the top rear of the action body, only the modified spur projecting above it.

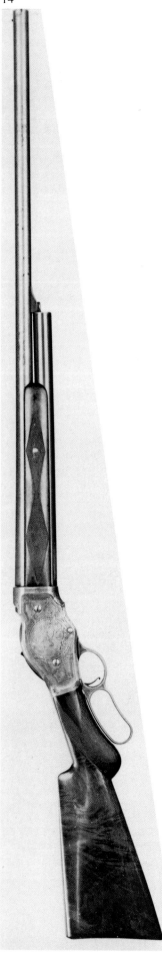

Number 6728 is a 12 gauge with 30 inch four blade Damascus barrel, more ornate outline engraving on the receiver sides and shoulders and top tang, and on the breech block and lever, a round vignette on the right side with prairie chicken shooting scene, deep scroll engraving on the entire action and most of the lever and hammer, fancy checked wood, and rubber butt plate—a truly remarkable piece, stunningly artistic by any standard.

Special Notes

1. A few guns after 50,000 had "Manufactured By The Winchester Repeating Arms Co. New Haven, Conn. U.S.A." (two lines) on the barrel. Some had the gauge stamped in large numerals near the receiver shoulder. Some later guns had the proof mark.

2. Firing pins on the first several thousand guns were retained by a screw visible on the top of the breech block. Later firing pin screws were inserted from the underside. Several design changes were phased in and may or may not be seen through a range of numbers from approximately 28,000, or 1889. Earlier forearm scales were held with one screw. Later ones had two. Earlier magazines were supported by a magazine tip screwed to a ramp which was brazed to the barrel. Later ones had a split band which clamped to the barrel. Earlier guns had left-hand extractors and cartridge guides on the right side. Later guns had left and right-hand extractors—most of them so stamped. Winchester advised the trade that the right-hand extractor would be installed on guns returned to the factory. Guns with right-hand extractors had a small screw just ahead of the large screw on the right hand side. The large screw stopped the breech bolt and the little screw pivoted the extractor up to engage chambered shells.

3. Some later triggers had smaller diameter curves. The first several thousand guns had steel butt plates with non slip designs. Then checked steel butt plates were used.

4. Barnes, et al. (1980, p. 32) indicated that the first production 10 gauge was number 22,148 in 1888. As number 6725 described above illustrated, special order 10 gauge guns were likely made before catalogs listed them. But, number 2217 is a 10 gauge with no extras. Was it a special order gun, just a serial number out of order, or a production gun completed much earlier than factory records indicated for the 10 gauge?

5. Some Model 1887's were made for the 70-150 cartridge. The 70 caliber 700- to 900-grain bullets, pushed by 150 grains of black powder made for tremendous recoil. Ratchet rifling was cut only near the muzzle. According to Madis (1981, p. 99) two of these guns are in England and one is in Pittsburgh, Pennsylvania.

6. Early 10 gauge forearm scales were the same length as 12 gauge scales, ten and one quarter inches. Later two-screw 10 gauge scales were one inch longer.

7. Nearly all receivers were color case hardened. Colors vary from near black through gray, blue, purple, and red to yellow. Some of the early gray case hardening appears to be nickel plating. It isn't. Plating was offered and is easy to distinguish. It flakes. Reputable experts believe that some receivers were factory blued.

8. As Madis (1981, p. 101) illustrated, some guns were factory equipped with sling rings bolted to the lower rear corner of the left side of the receiver. These were special ordered by American Express Company.

The Model 1887 was last listed in the March 1901 catalog. Prices were the same as shown above, but the last sentence on page 76 said, "Our stock of Lever Action Shotguns is exhausted, and we shall not be able to supply any of these

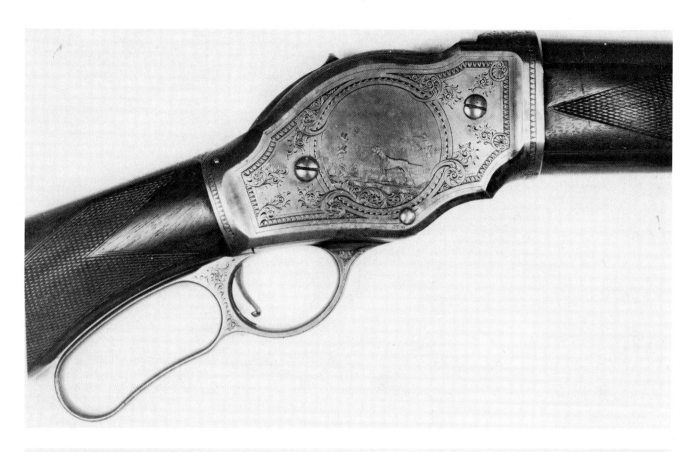

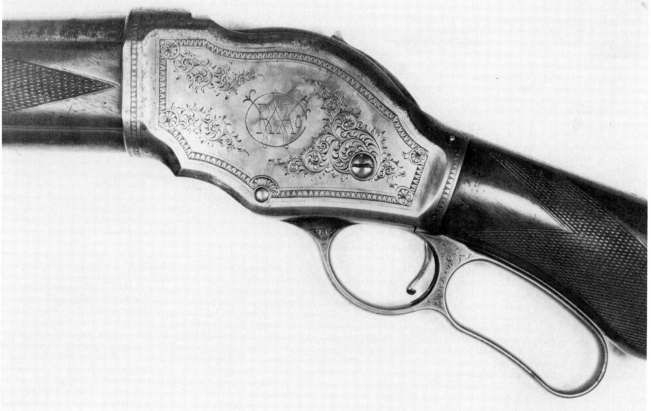

Left and above: Fancy Finished no. 6728, 12 ga., 30″ barrel, shipped March 3, 1888. This gun is discussed on p. 14. It is likely the most ornate Model 1887 extant.

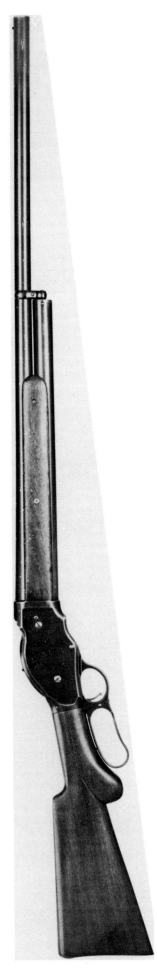

guns before late in the fall of 1901." Approximately 64,855 Model 1887's were made.

Model 1901/01 1901–1920

The January 1902 catalog was the first to describe the Model 1901.

The Model 1901 Winchester Lever Action Repeating Shotgun is the only 10 gauge repeater on the market. It is expressly bored to handle either smokeless or black powder, and is particularly well adapted for duck and wild-fowl shooting. This gun resembles in outline the original Winchester Lever Action Repeating Shotgun, but differs in detail. It has a tighter breech joint more completely supporting the shell in the chamber. A positive firing pin retractor is provided. The finger lever is made separate from the breech-block and with a finger lever lock. When the action is closed, the gun is locked against opening by this finger lever lock, but is instantly released by a downward pressure on the finger lever.

The standard gun is made with a 32 inch rolled steel barrel, hardened and browned frame, and pistol grip stock of plain walnut, not checked, finished with a checked steel butt plate. Barrels for this model are bored to shoot close and hard, and no gun will be sent out that does not make a good target. Unless otherwise specified, guns with 32 inch full choke barrels will be sent on all orders; but shorter barrels, or barrels with different styles of bore, either modified choke or full cylinder, will be furnished when so ordered without extra charge. Damascus barrels of different grades, and other extras, can be furnished at prices given below.

The stock of the Model 1901 Lever Action Repeating Shotgun is 12¾ inches long and has a drop of 1⅞ inch at the comb and 2⅜ inches at the heel. Special stocks, differing from the standard in length, or drop, or both, can be furnished at an extra cost.

The operation of the Model 1901 Lever Action Repeating Shotgun is simple, and can be easily understood. To load the magazine, throw down the lever and push five cartridges through the carrier into the magazine, placing the sixth in the chamber. The forward and backward motion of the finger lever, which can be executed while the gun is at the shoulder, throws out the empty shell, raises a new cartridge from the magazine and places it in the chamber, and the gun is then ready to be fired.

Price List Model 1901
10 Gauge Lever Action Repeating Shotgun

Winchester Model 1901, Repeating Shotgun, Lever Action 32 inch Rolled Steel Barrel, Pistol Grip Stock of Plain Walnut, Not Checked, 6 Shots, 10 Gauge only. Weight about 8¾ pounds.	$30.00

Extras For This Gun

Fancy Walnut Stock and Forearm, not checked,	$10.00
Checking Stock and Forearm,	$ 5.00
Extra Length or Drop of Stock, to order,	$10.00
Rubber Butt Plate, separate 80 cents, fitted to gun,	$ 2.00
Good (3 blade) Damascus Barrel in place of Rolled Steel Barrel (additional),	$15.00
Fine (4 blade) Damascus Barrel in place of Rolled Steel Barrel (additional),	$20.00

Plain Finished 1901–1920

The first Model 1901, number 64856, was delivered to the warehouse on August 27, 1901. Plain Finished guns were listed through catalog number 82. Catalog number 81, 1918 listed them at $38.00. No riot guns were listed in catalogs.

Fancy Finished 1901–1920

The January 1902 catalog showed a fancy finished gun with checking like that on the Model 1887 at $45.00. It did not have outline engraving. The 1916 catalog listed the Fancy Finished gun at $62.00. It had a 32 inch Rolled Steel Barrel and Fancy Walnut Pistol Grip Stock and Forearm and could be ordered with a rubber butt plate instead of steel. It did not have outline engraving.

Special Notes

1. Catalogs indicated that receivers were browned. Madis (1981, p.104) indicated that prior to about 67,000 a niter-bluing process resulted in a shallow blue and that thereafter rust blue (called browning) resulted in a more durable finish.

2. Barrels had complete markings ending with Model 1901 10 GA. They were proof marked. The upper tang was marked "—Winchester—Trade Mark" (two lines) until about 71,500. Then they were marked "Reg. In U.S. Pat. OFF—Winchester—Trade Mark—" (three lines).

3. The January 1913 catalog listed Damascus barrels. The 1914 and 1916 catalogs did not. They listed Silver's Recoil Pad @ $7.00 and a canvas gun cover @ $2.00.

4. On page 21 of the April 1981 *Winchester Collector*, Lewis E. Yearout reported the whereabouts of number 64856. It has the 32 and 1/16 inch barrel, 10 gauge marking on the barrel, and proof mark. It does not have the model or trade mark stamps anywhere.

The 1918 catalog designated the model as 01. The Model 01 was discontinued in 1920 after approximately 13,500 of the Model 1901/01 had been made.

The gun at left is Model 1901 Plain Finished no. 70362, 10 ga., 30″, shipped from the factory July 26, 1906.

The .70-150 cartridge at right is best known for appearance on the Winchester 1889 "Big W" cartridge display board. This specimen has a wood spacer in the case and two holes drilled in the opposite side through which it was wired to the board. The rather thick head is flat and bears no headstamp. Winchester made a very few Model 1887's for this bulleted load with ratchet rifling extending a short distance back from the muzzle. This same idea was patented by George Vincent Fosbery in Great Britain in 1886. Gunmakers Holland & Holland bought the rights and produced guns with this system under the name "Paradox," for shooting either short, lead projectiles or bird shot. Some .70-150 cartridges have thin rims. It is difficult to assess authenticity of specimens other than those from cartridge boards because replicas have been fashioned from 12 gauge brass shotshells.

W.R.A. Co. RIVAL empty shotshells were brown. Gauges, year introduced, and year discontinued were: 10, 1894–1897; 12, 1884–1897; 14, 1890–1897; 16, 1890–1897; 20, 1890–1897. The 10, 12, 14, and 16 gauge Rivals were offered loaded from 1894 to 1897. The box label is black on cream.

Metal Lined shells were much higher quality than their predecessors. They were made in various shades of green and were offered empty as follows: 4, 1897–1907; 8, 1897–1907; 10, 1894–1907; 12, 1897–1907. Loaded 10 and 12 gauge Metal Lined shells were offered from 1894 to 1907. The base of the shell was lined with metal on the inside. For a time beginning in 1901, Metal Lined and other empty shells had "1901" at the top of the headstamp instead of "WINCHESTER."

Blue Rival empties were offered as follows: 10, 1894–1904; 12, 1894–1904; 14, 1896–1904; 16, 1894–1904; 20, 1896–1904. These shells were also offered loaded from 1894 to 1903. The label on this 8½-inch square, 100-round box is cream with black lettering.

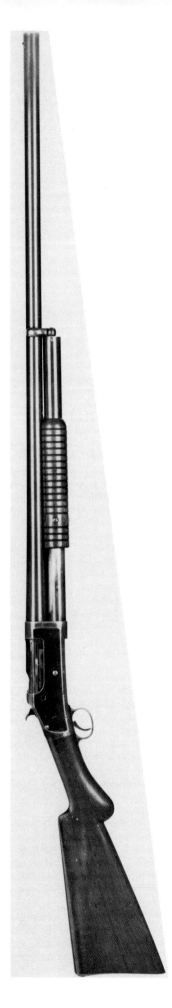

Chapter 4

MODELS 1893 AND 1897/97

Model 1893   1893–1897

The Model 1893 was announced in the June 1893 catalog. It was the first slide action shotgun produced by Winchester, introduced to compete with the Burgess and other slide action guns. It entailed minor improvements over a Browning Brothers' patent purchased in 1890. The June 1893 catalog noted:

> This gun is operated by a sliding forearm below the barrel. It is locked by the closing motion and can be unlocked only by pushing forward the firing pin, which may be done by the hammer or by the finger. When the hammer is down, the backward and forward motion or the sliding forearm unlocks and opens the breech block, ejects the cartridge or fired shell and replaces it with a fresh cartridge.
>
> The construction of the arm is such that the hammer cannot fall or the firing pin strike the cartridge until the breech block is in place and locked fast. The trigger touches the sear only when the gun is closed—that is, the hammer cannot be let down except when the gun is locked. Having closed the gun and set the hammer at half-cock, it is locked both against opening and pulling the trigger. While the hammer stands at the full-cock notch, the gun is locked against opening.

This statement was changed slightly and inserted between pages 48 and 49 of the October 1893 catalog. This catalog overstated design features of the Model 93:

> Many of our correspondents having asked us to make a shotgun with the sliding fore-arm movement, we now offer our Model 1893, which we believe will be found to fill all the requirements of such an arm. It is safe, quick, and easy of manipulation from the shoulder, simple in construction, and sure in operation, easy to load and unload. Its moving parts are few and strong. . . The best material, made especially for us, is used. We make all our forgings and use no castings. All parts are interchangeable, and every precaution has been taken in material and workmanship which long and great experience, perfected machinery and skilled labor enables. The Winchester rolled steel barrel, which has added so greatly to the success which the Winchester (lever) shotgun has attained, will of course be used.

Catalogs did not use terms such as "standard" and fancy finished. However, catalogs from March 1897 showed plain and fancy finished guns. That is to say, variations will occur, depending upon which of the following were ordered:

Winchester Repeating Shot Gun, Model 1893 rolled steel barrel, with plain pistol grip stock 30 or 32 inch barrel, 12 gauge	$25.00
Fancy Walnut Stock and Fore-arm, not checked, extra	10.00
Checking Stock,	5.00
Extra Length or Drop of Stock, to order	10.00
Rubber Butt Plate,	2.00

Good (3 blade) Damascus Barrel in place of rolled steel barrel (additional),	15.00
Fine (4 blade) Damascus Barrel in place of rolled steel barrel (additional)	20.00

These prices pertained throughout the Model 1893's short history and the beginning of the 1897's. A gun with four-blade Damascus barrel, fancy walnut stock, checking, and rubber butt was shown in the catalog at $62.00. Modified choke or cylinder bore barrels were furnished on special order. The magazine held 5 shells. Only 12 gauge guns were made. A large 12 was stamped on barrels near the receiver, and all had 2⅝ inch chambers. All slide handles shown in catalogs were corrugated. The 30 inch gun weighed approximatly 7¾ pounds. After number 12,300, action slides were stamped Winchester Model 1893—two lines.

The March 1897 catalog contained extra lines of type which read: "Send for our handsomely illustrated 24-page catalogue showing the engraving and checking on fancy guns." There were factory engraved Model 1893's. Lew Yearout reported that B25523 had a rolled steel barrel, checked forearm, checked stock with hard rubber grip cap and butt plate, and 12 inch pull, light scroll engraving, and "Marta J. Munson" on the left side.

The gun on p. 20 is Model 1893 no. 8381, 12 ga., 32" barrel.

The action was adequate for black powder loads and inadequate for smokeless powder loads, which became popular in the 1890's. According to Madis (1981, p. 132), after the Model 1897 was introduced, Winchester offered to trade a Model 1897 for any 1893 returned to the factory. Of course, returned guns were destroyed—I should wager after recovering parts useable in 1897's. It can be argued that the Model 1893 was rushed into production. But, Winchester's thinking at the time centered on *improvement*. The firm assumed that lines of products were evolving, e.g., lever action rifles, lever action shotguns, slide action rifles, slide action shotguns.

The December 1896 catalog contained an extra sentence: "This gun will use any load of smokeless powder which can be properly loaded in a 2⅝ inch, 12 gauge shell." The March 1897 catalog did not have this sentence. Page 78 of the November 1897 catalog described Models 1893 and 1897 and indicated that the 1897 was "made expressly to shoot either black or nitro powder equally well." This catalog did not picture 1893's. It appears to have been Winchester's way of smoothing transition to a stronger gun. Approximately 34,050 of the Model 1893 were made.

Special Notes

1. Madis (1981, p. 132) described number B 29817 with a twenty-two inch barrel. Catalogs did not usually list such riot guns. However, because Model 1887 guard and riot guns were furnished on special order and later as catalog items, it is altogether likely that orders for riot guns in the later models were honored (the March 1898 catalog listed 1887 and 1897 riot guns).

2. There is some confusion about Winchester slide action rifles and shotguns firing on closing if the trigger was held back. This was normal for Models 1890 through 62 (61 included) and Models 1893 through 1912/12. None would fire before battery. However, all had what some users thought to be the advantage of firing upon closing if the trigger was held back. No faster repeaters could be made. Exhibition shooters demonstrated this. Some of them, excellent field shots, perfected the technique of holding the trigger back and closing the action just as the barrel came into proper alignment with the target.

3. Some Model 1893's had serial numbers obliterated and "W.R.A. Co." stamped in their place. This was likely done by chain stores which violated fair trade price stipulations made by Winchester and did not want guns traced.

Mechanical Changes to Models 1893 and 1897

A large number of mechanical changes were made. George Madis was very kind to send me material from factory files which describe many of these. Evidently, the first guns were made in accord with the Browning design as modified by a Mr. Libbens. The following is from the material as I received it.

LIST OF CHANGES MADE IN THE MODEL 1893 DURING ITS PERIOD OF MANUFACTURE.

During the period of making the first 13,000:
A left-hand cartridge stop was put in.

In September, 1894, after about 13,000 had been made, the following changes were made: The guns were marked with the letter "A" above the serial number.

1st   Action slide lock placed in the side of the carrier. (Recoil lock)

2nd   Stop for action handle was put on the magazine in the form of a collar.

3rd   A trigger adjusting screw was put in guard.

In January 1897, after about 32,800 had been made, the following changes were made. The guns were marked with a letter "B" over the serial number.

1st   New cartridge guide (not flat)

2nd   Left-hand yielding extractor inserted in bolt.

LIST OF CHANGES BETWEEN THE MODEL 1893 AND THE MODEL 1897 REPEATING SHOTGUN.

In June, 1897, after about 34,000 shotguns Model 1893 had been made, the following changes were made. Then the gun was called the Model 1897, the serial numbers of the guns continuing.

1st   Top of cartridge ejecting opening in frame made straight.

2nd   Spring placed on inside of action handle encircling the magazine.

3rd   Release pin and plunger (for action slide lock).

4th   New firing pin lock put in breech block.

5th   Friction spring put in under cartridge guide.

6th   Collar put inside of magazine to keep spring and follower from coming out.

7th   Screw put in receiver to hold magazine from turning.

8th   Receiver holding bolt made shorter.

Standard or Plain Finished takedown no. D327225, 16 ga., 28″, shipped May 29, 1906. Factory refinished circa 1960 with late wood and Winchester recoil pad.

9th   Butt stock made longer. Drop changed, and outside shape changed slightly.

10th   Top of breech block made straight.

In February, 1898, after about 47,000 shotguns had been made, some changes were made in the Model 1897. Then the gun was marked with the letter "C" over the serial number.

1st   A small wire was put into the receiver and connected to the action slide lock release pin, to hold it from coming out when the gun was taken apart.

2nd   Receiver made 1½ hundredths thicker on each side. This was thought best on account of the increased cuts on the inside.

3rd   Action slide lock spring changed.

In April, 1898, after about 50,000 shotguns had been made (Models 1893 and 1897), some changes were made, and the Model 1897 detachable barrel and magazine put on the market.

Additional changes were made. The first Model 1897's had no ejector spring. (The ejector was a little block pinned to the receiver wall.) "C" guns had the ejector spring. I do not know whether all "B" Model 1893 and 1897 guns did. "C" guns had rounded end magazine plugs. The end of the magazine plug was flat on "D" guns. "E" guns had slightly deeper 5/16″ wide grooves on the receiver ring. Prior to the "E" guns, cartridge stops were fastened with screws through the receiver sides and shells were difficult to release from the magazine for unloading—most shooters worked them through the action. This was changed by fastening the cartridge stops with screws through the bottom of the action and providing buttons which could be pushed to retract the cartridge stops. These are not all of the changes. Madis (1981, p. 168) stated that 37 major and 52 minor changes were made in the first twelve years of production of the Model 1897.

Pigeon shells were very similar to Metal lined shells, but had paper base wads. They were light green and were offered in 10 and 12 gauge empty or loaded from 1898 to 1907.

Model 1897/97, 1897–1957

The November 1897 catalog introduced the Model 1897 in glowing terms.

The great success which has attended the sale of the Model 1893 Repeating Shot Gun has led us to offer a new form of this gun, which it has seemed best, by reason of many changes and improvements, to call the Model 1897, although the users of the previous Model 1893 will recognize in it many points of similarity. The old form of sliding fore-end, breech-block, carrier-block, hammer, and trigger have been retained, but in the detail many alterations are collected together in the Model 1897 gun.

The frame has been altered to use a 2¾ inch shell as well as a 2⅝ inch. The frame at the top has been covered over so that the ejecting of the shell is now entirely from the side. This adds great strength to the frame, and permits the use, without danger of jamming, of a 2¾ inch shell.

A new lock opening by recoil, or otherwise at the will of the operator, has been put upon the gun. Under the slide handle, and acting against the stop of the magazine, is placed a spring. When the gun is closed, this spring pushes against the upper end of the action slide, and presses it toward the stock. A lever is hung in the carrier-block, when the slide handle is pressed forward, a spring in the rear end of the lever forces the forward end of the lever out and it catches against the notch in the action slide. While the hammer stands at full cock, the rear end of the lever is forced outward and its notched forward end holds the slide fast.

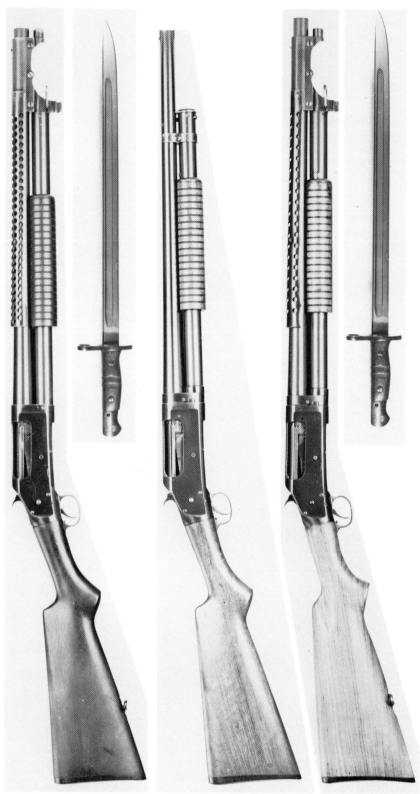

From left—Trench gun, solid frame no. E684452, 12 ga., 20″, shipped April 30, 1918.

Riot gun, takedown no. E646651, 12 ga., 20″, February 9, 1917.

Trench gun, takedown no. E956146, 12 ga., 20″, February 24, 1941.

When the hammer stands at half cock, the same occurs. But when the hammer has fallen, the spring which lies under the rear end of the lever forces the forward end of the lever toward the center of the gun. The spring under the slide handle, however, still holds the forward end of the lever in place, and the gun cannot be opened until a slight forward motion of the slide handle releases the lever. Thereupon it may be opened by pulling back the slide handle. In firing, the recoil of the gun gives the slight forward motion to the slide handle, releases the lever, and enables the immediate opening of the gun. It results from this that the gun awaits the explosion of the cartridge before opening. If the shell hangs fire, the gun will not come open in the hands of an operator who is holding back upon the slide handle with the intention of making a quick second shot. It will, however, come immediately open when the recoil of the gun occurs.

To open the gun at full cock, a button upon the right hand side must be pressed. This throws off the recoil lock and allows the gun to come open by making a slight forward push of the slide handle. When the hammer has fallen without exploding the cartridge, it will be necessary to push forward the slide handle before the gun can be pulled open. At half cock the gun is locked against firing and opening.

Double extractors are furnished. That on the left hand side guides the bolt, enabling it to be fitted close in the frame so that a tight breech joint obtains.

Upon the right side of the carrier block a movable cartridge guide is placed. The motion of this guide is so great that, in connection with the overhang of the frame, the slide opening of the gun is completely covered at the movement when the cartridge is lifted from the magazine by the carrier-block. This prevents the escape of the shell when the gun is turned sideways in the act of loading.

A new firing-pin lock is also furnished, acting at the first opening motion of the carrier, so that the firing-pin stands locked at all times, except when the gun is closed and ready to fire. The arrangement of the firing-pin lock is such that the firing-pin is always free at the time of firing, and the hammer has no other work to do than the moving of the firing-pin. The firing pin is made lighter than in the Model 1893 gun. This enables a lighter mainspring in its turn, with shorter and lighter trigger pull.

Two cartridge stops are furnished, one on each side opposite the mouth of the magazine. These carry the weight of the cartridges and the magazine spring equally at two opposite points on the head of the cartridge so that the cartridge is not deformed about the head from pounding in the magazine.

A longer stock with less drop has been put upon this gun, which it is believed will suit the market better than the old form of short and crooked stock which has been heretofore used. The length of stock is 13¾ inches; the drop at comb, 1⅝ inches; drop at heel, 2½ inches.

This gun will hereafter be furnished in place of the Model 1893 upon all orders.

The standard gun will be made up with rolled steel barrel, blued frame, and pistol grip stock of plain wood, not checked. All guns will be full choked, and no gun will be sent out which will not make a good target. Guns with cylinder bore or modified choke will be furnished to order.

The standard length of barrel will be 30 or 32 inches, as may be desired. But, unless otherwise ordered, guns with 30 inch barrels will in all cases be sent.

Two kinds of Damascus barrels will be furnished when desired. . . .

The standard gun will have a stock 13¾ inches in length, 1⅝ inch drop at comb, and 2½ inches drop at heel. If so ordered, guns will be furnished with Model 1893 stocks 13 inches in length, having a drop of 1¾ inches at comb and 2¾ inches at heel, without extra charge. Any variation from these standard lengths or drops will be charged for extra.

Fancy Finished no. E492425, 12 ga., 30″, June 28, 1910. This gun has a checked grip, plain forearm, and Hawkins recoil pad.

Standard, Plain Finished or Field, 1897 to 1957

The standard gun was offered in several variations in addition to the standard barrel lengths and chokes. It was first listed at $25.00. Perhaps the most interesting of these is the brush gun, available from November 1897 to 1931. Brush guns had shorter stocks with more drop and 26 inch barrels. They were first listed at $27.00. The solid frame brush gun had a shorter magazine which held only four shells. It weighed slightly less than seven pounds. The take down brush gun had the regular magazine. This gun could be had after 1931 but it was no longer designated "Brush" in catalogs.

The standard grade was available in the riot variation (12 gauge 20 inch cylinder bore) in solid frame from 1897 to 1935 and in take down from 1921 to 1957.

The standard grade was first listed in the trench variation in solid frame in the 1920 catalog. It had previously been sold to the military for use in Europe in WWI. Trench guns were the same as riot guns but with bayonet studs, usually handguards, and sling swivels. In 1935 the solid frame was discontinued and the takedown trenchgun was added. It was discontinued in 1945. The takedown Model 97 and Model 12 trench guns are odd because, with the bayonet stud attached, the takedown feature serves no purpose. Brush, riot, and trench guns were all 12 gauge.

Fancy Finished 1897 to 1913

The grade had a checked grip and a corrugated forearm. With four-blade Damascus barrel, fancy walnut stock, pistol grip checked, and checked rubber butt plate it was first listed at $62.00. It was shown in Catalog No. 78, January 1913 and was not in Catalog No. 79, 1914.

Trap Gun 1897 to 1931: 12 & 16 gauge

This gun had a 30 inch rolled steel barrel, selected fancy walnut hand made stock, straight checked grip with oil finish and black diamonds in the grip, and checked rubber butt plate. It was first listed at $47.00. "TRAP GUN" was engraved on the breech block and it could be had with a matted barrel. Within certain limits, purchasers could specify stock dimensions. Solid frame and takedown trap guns were made. After 1926, "TRAP GUN" was not always engraved on the breech block.

Tournament Gun 1910 to 1931: 12 gauge only

This gun was specially designated for trap shooting. It was first listed at $42.00. It had the same features as the trap gun, except that the wood was not as fancy and it was furnished only with standard dimensions. The stock could be ordered shorter than standard for $2.00.

Trap Gun, solid frame no. C226873, 12 ga., 28″, shipped December 1, 1903. It has a checked straight grip, plain forearm, and Winchester pad added later.

Pigeon Gun 1897 to 1939: 12 and 16 gauge

This gun had full fancy checked wood with black diamonds in the grip. PIGEON GUN was engraved on the breech block. The standard barrel length was 28 inches, and the barrel was matted. It was profusely engraved with a quail shooting scene on the right and a live bird shooting scene on the left. This was a made-to-order gun, first listed at $100.00. Many features, such as matted barrels, pistol grip stocks, 30- and 32-inch barrels, and various brands of recoil pads will be found on these guns. After 1926, "PIGEON GUN" was not always engraved on the breech block.

Standard Trap Gun 1931 to 1939: 12 and 16 gauge

This gun replaced the tournament gun and the trap gun. It had a beavertail forearm and a longer butt stock with less drop and the Winchester recoil pad (other brands on special order). It did not have black diamonds.

Special Trap Gun 1931 to 1939: 12 and 16 gauge

In catalogs this gun looks like the older trap grade with rubber butt plate and black diamonds. Perhaps the printers used an old engraving to save the expense of a new one. On the other hand, it may have been produced exactly like the pictures, having been given a little more elaborate name. It was a made-to-order gun like the original trap gun.

Special Notes

1. The large number of options make collecting the 1897 especially interesting. At some times special engraving and wood could be ordered on any grade. A good case in point is Lew Yearout's C183538, which is pictured in Madis (1977) on page 630. This gun has a 28 inch full choke Damascus barrel, corrugated forearm, full fancy butt stock with rubber grip cap and butt plate, light engraving on the left side with an Irish setter and his name "Tim" in capitals, and "F.E.L." on the right side.

2. Matted barrels were available on early guns. I assume this did not include brush, riot, and trench guns. But I would not be surprised to find a solid frame brush gun with this and/or other options. Matted barrels could be ordered on standard guns as could shorter stocks, checking, fancier wood with or without checking, etc. I also assume that matted barrels were available on the pigeon gun until it was discontinued. I doubt that any standard or special trap guns had matted barrels.

3. The receivers on trap, tournament, pigeon, standard trap and special trap guns had a matted groove.

4. Damascus barrels were discontinued in 1914. From the start, full and modified chokes and cylinder bores were offered. Improved cylinder and improved modified were offered in 1931. Skeet 1 and skeet 2 were first listed in 1940. Yes, there are Model 97 skeet guns in this sense, but there was not a skeet grade designation.

5. All 12 gauge guns have 2¾ inch chambers. The 16 gauge was introduced in 1900 with 2⅝ inch chambers. This was changed to 2¾ inch in 1931. The 16 gauge was last listed in 1950. Madis (1981, p. 167) indicated that some remained

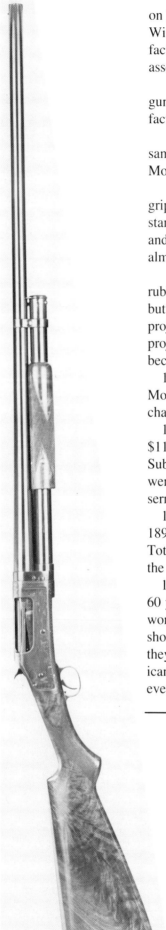

on hand until 1959. I have examined 16 gauge serial number D327225. It has a Winchester recoil pad and wood shaped like the last 12 gauge guns. It may be factory refinished with new wood. On the other hand, it could have been assembled from left over parts.

6. Madis (1981, p. 167) stated that experiments were made with 20 gauge guns. No production 20 gauge guns were made, and it is unlikely that any left the factory.

7. It is interesting to note that 12 and 16 gauge Model 97's were built on the same frame. The same was true of 16, 20, and 28 gauge Model 12's as well as Model 21's in 20, 28 gauge and 410 bore, and the Model 24 in 16 and 20 gauge.

8. The half pistol grip became standard on the Model 97 in 1908. Straight grips were standard on trap, tournament, and pigeon guns. Pistol grips were standard on the standard trap and special trap. In 1947, the wood for field grade and riot was changed to full pistol grip with flat bottom and the large forearm with almost flat bottom.

9. Early plain finished guns had smooth steel butt plates. From the start, rubber butt plates could be special ordered. Some trench guns had checked steel butt plates. There were three types of rubber butt plates: the first had a curved projection going about ⅜ inch into the comb; the second was similar without the projection; the third was plastic, distinguishable from Model 12 butt plates because it was thicker.

10. Until approximately 550,000, the action slide was marked "Winchester Model 1897" in several different configurations. The model designation was changed to 97 in 1918. Guns with no marking on the action slide are Model 97's.

11. The January 2, 1930 Retail Price List listed "Stainless Steel Barrels" at $11.75 extra.The 1931 catalog listed this option for plain and matted barrels. Subsequent literature did not show this option. Several different checking patterns were applied to the hammers. The last guns had hammers which were simply serrated.

12. Model 1893 and 1897 serial numbers were consecutive. The first Model 1897 was 34,151. John M. Olin was presented serial number 1,000,000 in 1951. Total production was approximately 1,024,700; however, guns assembled from the last remaining parts might have slightly higher numbers.

13. The Model 97 far and away outsold its competitors, was in production for 60 years, and was as reliable as any gun made in its day, or now. It was hard to work because there were several long and close fitting bearing surfaces. Many shooters used reloaded shells the gun had to practically resize to chamber, and they seldom cleaned or lubricated the important surfaces. Several Grand American winners used Model 97's and so did Mrs. Topperwein, the best lady shooter ever. It served the market hunter better than any other mass-produced gun.

Pigeon Gun, takedown no. C139059, 12 ga., 32″, June 15, 1901.

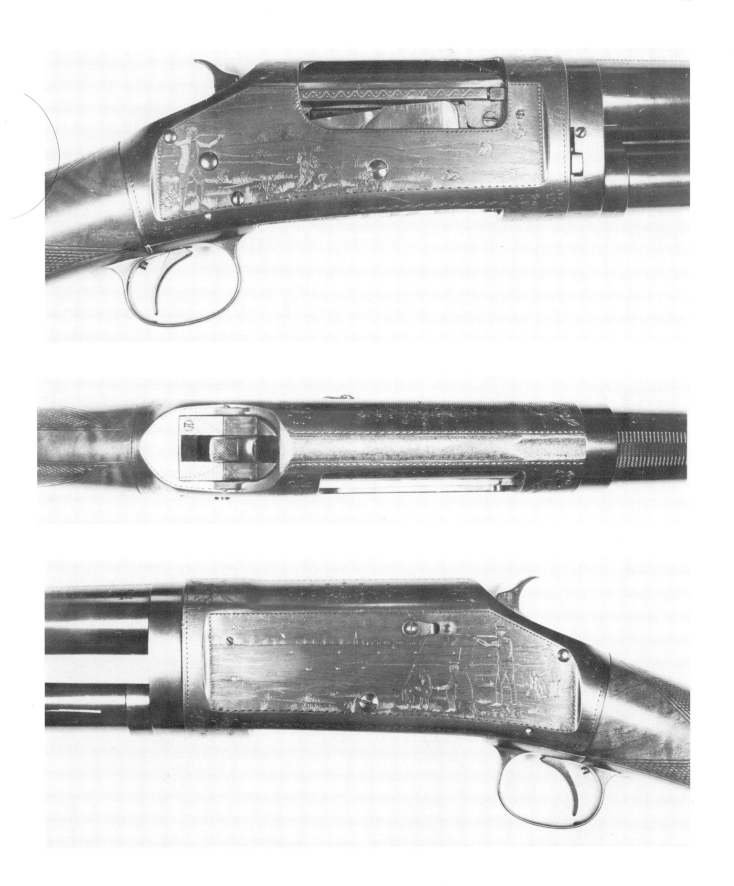

Engraving detail on the Model 97 Pigeon Gun.

SLIDE ACTION COMPETITORS OF WINCHESTER

Left—Spencer slide action shotgun, 12 ga., 32″, made in Windsor, Connecticut by Spencer Arms Company from 1882 to 1889. Francis Bannerman made very similar guns under Spencer patents in Brooklyn, New York from 1890 to approximately 1907. In 1894, Bannerman brought suit against Philip G. Sanford, New York agent for Winchester, charging that the Model 1893 and the Model 1890 rifle infringed on the April 21, 1885 patent of Sylvester H. Roper, former partner of Christopher M. Spencer (Spencer invented a repeating rifle and an automatic screw machine). The court decided in Winchester's favor largely because Winchester proved that working slide action guns had been patented in Europe prior to the 1885 Roper patent.

Right—Burgess slide action shotgun, 12 ga., 30″, man ictured by the Burgess Gun Company of Buffalo, New York from 1892 to 1898. Winchester bought the machines, tools, fixtures and patents of the Burgess Gun Company in September 1899. So far as could be determined from Winchester records, no use was made of Burgess patents and the guns were not sold by Winchester. Note that this shotgun is operated by a slide which is integral with the grip. This model took down into two pieces. Burgess also used a folding takedown feature, which in a short-barreled version was marketed as a bank guard gun or under-the-coat gun for policemen.

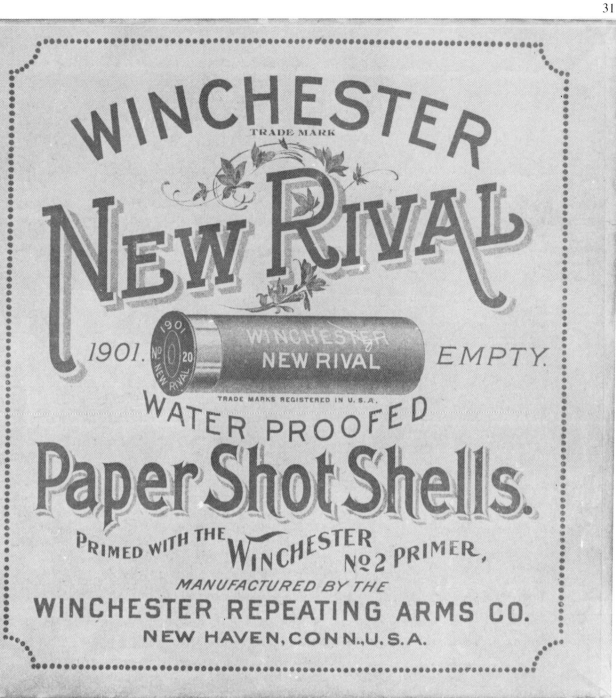

New Rival olive green shells were offered empty and loaded in 10, 12, 14, 16, and 20 gauges from 1897 to 1920, except the 14 gauge which was not loaded after 1917. The cream box label is printed in green, measures 7⅛″ square.

32

The 25-round boxes on this page labeled for loaded New Rival shells had the same color scheme as the 100-round specimen for primed empties. Note the emphasis given the wads.

Two unusual New Rival light green shells are shown. The first was evidently a salesman's or exhibition shooter's sample. The other, though professionally done, was probably hand loaded by the owner of a European-made ball-and-shot gun or double rifle. Such loads were never listed by Winchester.

In 1920 New Rival paper was changed to blue. All blue New Rivals had one corrugation as did some of the olive green ones. Some empties had the 1901 headstamp. New Rival shells were offered until 1917 in 14 gauge; 1927 in 10, 16 and 20 gauges; 1929 in 12 gauge. Shown are a factory load and the rare empty with sunburst around the primer. The box label print is blue on white with WINCHESTER and NEW RIVAL in red.

Yellow Rival shells were offered empty only in 10, 12, 14, 16 and 20 gauges from 1899 to 1904. The 14 and 16 gauge shells are rare today.

Nublack loaded shells were listed from 1905 to 1938 in 10, 12, 16 and 20 gauges. For some periods smaller gauge Nublack and New Rival shells were loaded in Repeater grade shells. The 24 and 28 gauge Nublack shells were likely offered from 1911 through 1921. The cream label has WINCHESTER in red, the other print in black.

The last Nublack box (below) is known in 10, 12 and 16 gauges. It has a green border with red and black lettering on white. The ducks in flight are in full color. Nublack shells were also sold empty in 10, 12, 16 and 20 gauges from 1927 to 1937. Most Nublack shells were yellow but some loaded shells and empties in small gauges were red.

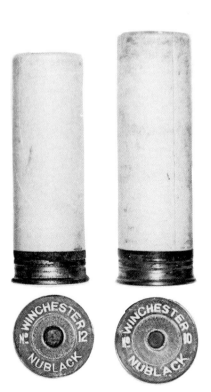

Chapter 5

BREECH-LOADING CANNON

The Cannon was first listed in the March 1903 catalog. It was developed and patented by Charles H. Griffith, a Winchester employee. Employees dubbed it the Model 1898 sometime after it was introduced. The catalog description read:

WINCHESTER BREECH LOADING CANNON
(BLANKS ONLY.)
FOR SALUTING AND CELEBRATING.

This cannon has been designed to supply a general demand for a low-priced breech-loading cannon possessing safety, simplicity of construction, and ease of manipulation. All these desirable features are combined in this gun. In it can be used either paper or brass shells, and we recommend our 10 gauge Winchester shells loaded with 9 drams of black powder, with two Black Edge and One Card wad, to produce the loudest report. This cannon has so few parts that it cannot readily get out of order or cause any trouble in its operation. It can be easily dismounted if necessary.

DESCRIPTION: This cannon consists of a 12 inch tapered, rolled-steel barrel, cylinder bored, mounted on a shapely cast iron carriage, substantially built, which is supplied with two heavy wheels at the forward end 3⅝ inches in diameter. The barrel and breech closure are proved and tested to withstand a much greater pressure than can be developed by any charge of BLACK POWDER that can be loaded in a 10 gauge shell. The carriage and wheels are nicely japanned, the barrel blued, and breech closure hardened black, giving the gun a very neat appearance. The length of the cannon over all is 17 inches, its height 7¼ inches, and its width 7 inches.

OPERATION: The cannon is opened (1) by pushing down the hammer, (2) pulling up the breech-bolt handle, and (3) letting down the breech-bolt, thus exposing the chamber. The shell can then be inserted and the gun closed in the reverse order. The breech-bolt is so constructed that the gun cannot be fired until it is locked, thus insuring its safety. To fire the gun, the hammer is pulled forward by a quick pull on a cord which is passed through the hole in the rear of the hammer, drilled for that purpose. A proper extractor is provided for extracting the fired shell. The mainspring is made of sufficient strength to avoid missfires. The barrel can be raised or lowered by an elevating screw placed underneath it.

This cannon will be found satisfactory for Fourth of July and other celebrations, and for saluting. As the shells used in it are not expensive, almost anybody can afford to own one. Both the cannon and 10 gauge Winchester shell (paper or brass) can be procured of all dealers.

PRICE LIST.

12 inch, 10 gauge, rolled steel, cylinder bored, blued barrel, cast iron frame. Weight about 14 pounds	$7.00
Blank cartridges, 10 gauge, 9 drams black powder, per 1000	$30.00

The breech-loading cannon with blued finish and iron wheels (above). The chromium plated model with rubber tire wheels was introduced in 1931.

Special Notes

1. The Winchester Breech Loading Cannon underwent very few changes in its 60 years. Early cannons were shipped in dovetailed pine boxes, sized and labeled especially for them. A lanyard, i.e., a length of cord, was provided for firing the cannon from a distance to the rear. They had "-NOT FOR BALL-" rolled on the barrel ahead of the trunnion and "MANUFACTURED BY THE WINCHESTER REPEATING ARMS CO. NEW HAVEN. CONN. U.S.A. PAT. AUG. 20. 1901 10 GA." (two lines) on the top of the breech. Muzzles measured one inch and breeches measured 2⅛ inches. Barrels were 12 inches long.

2. The first alteration increased the muzzle diameter to 1¼ inch. This occurred about 1907.

3. The next alterations moved the roll to about 45° on the right side of the breech, enlarged "NOT FOR BALL" leaving off the dashes, added "WINCHESTER TRADE MARK REG. U.S. PAT. OFF. & FGN," at about 45° on the left side of the breech, and added a proof mark on top of the barrel. These occurred about 1911.

4. An option was introduced in 1931. The japanned carriage and blued barrel style was continued and a chromium plated style with small rubber tires was introduced. They were listed at $18.00 and $35.00.

5. Post World War II cannons were identical, except that at some point the tires on the chromium finished style were made much larger with the "Firestone" trademark. The July 1, 1954 Component Parts List showed the small tires; the December 30, 1955 Wholesale-Retail Price List showed the Firestone tires. Some post World War II catalogs did not list cannons. The last one to do so was the January 2, 1958 issue. The black finish, metal wheels style was listed at $69.95 and the chromium plated, rubber tires style was $129.20.

6. Cannons were not serially marked. Mating numbers were stamped on the major parts. It is likely that batches of several hundred were made as demand warranted. Export cannons had serial numbers stamped on the carriage sides.

The cannon was discontinued in January 1958 after approximately 18,400 were made.

Bellmore-Johnson Cannons

In 1976, the Bellmore-Johnson Tool Company of Hamden, Conn., was licensed to make cannons. These replicas had "WRA Co." on both sides of the carriage and "Mfg. by the Bellmore-Johnson Tool Co., Hamden, Ct., under license from Winchester Div., Olin Corp." on the barrel. Cannons were made in black, chromium, and solid brass styles. Machining and finish on the black and chromium ones were rough. The brass ones were nicely done, but they were not made in New Haven. Serious collectors maintain that a complete collection may be assembled without these replicas.

Two of the shotshells which were made up as black powder blanks.

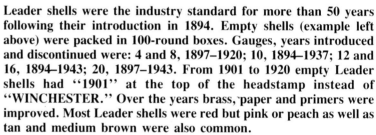

Leader shells were the industry standard for more than 50 years following their introduction in 1894. Empty shells (example left above) were packed in 100-round boxes. Gauges, years introduced and discontinued were: 4 and 8, 1897–1920; 10, 1894–1937; 12 and 16, 1894–1943; 20, 1897–1943. From 1901 to 1920 empty Leader shells had "1901" at the top of the headstamp instead of "WINCHESTER." Over the years brass, paper and primers were improved. Most Leader shells were red but pink or peach as well as tan and medium brown were also common.

The box above is believed to be the first for loaded Leader shells. Brand names of the smokeless powders used were profuse and important to shooters. The box label is cream with red lettering. Gauges, years of introduction and discontinuance for loaded Leader shells were: 8, 1900–1921; 10, 1894–1938; 12, 1894–1943; 16, 1894–1943; 20, 1900–1943. Leader 8 gauge shells were also loaded with black powder from 1907 to 1921. The 12 gauge specimen in center above came from the box.

The rare specimen at left is a Leader shell specially headstamped for Adam H. Bogardus, who was a match and exhibition shooter from the 1870's to the early 1900's. The headstamp means "Captain A. Bogardus, Champion." He gave himself both titles but did beat other name shooters of the day.

This box, introduced around 1900, has a red on white label with some print in blue, trim and lightning burst in gold.

John Gardner, Superintendent of the Cartridge Department, was granted patent no. 25611 for circular grooves or corrugations around the metal base of the shell in 1896. The first Leader with corrugations had three. In 1903 a fourth corrugation was added.

Leader Brush shells are rare. Gauges, years of introduction and discontinuance were: 12, 1905–1921; 16, 1905–1921; 20, 1913–1921.

Primed empty Leaders were provided in several lengths. The specimen at right is 4″.

The 1901 LEADER No. 8 is self explanatory. It was a banquet favor at the Bristol (New Hampshire) Gun Club on January 20, 1916. There are almost no commemorative Winchester shells.

Leader shells with DuPont Oval progressive burning powder were loaded in 10, 12, 16 and 20 gauges from 1925 to 1927. Then the catalog listing was "loaded with progressive burning smokeless powders such as Oval, Herco, and D. X." In 1933 Leader Super Speed shells replaced these. Leader lacquered shells (below) were introduced in 1929 and discontinued in 1937. The label is white and red on a blue background.

In 1933 Leader Super Speed shells replaced the earlier listing of progressive powder Leader shells. The 10 gauge size was discontinued in 1938, 16 and 20 gauge in 1943, and 12 gauge in 1947. A 12 gauge magnum shell was introduced in 1939 and discontinued in 1947. The box is cream with red and blue print.

The rare box below appeared on the 1942 price list. Examples for 12 and 16 gauge shells exist. The background is yellow and red with red and blue print.

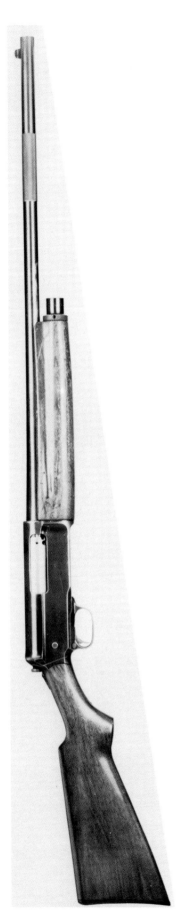

Chapter 6
MODEL 1911/11

The Model 1911 was introduced in the October 1911 catalog. The first guns were delivered to the warehouse on October 7, 1911. The regular pages described the guns and a four page insert explained how to disassemble the gun and change barrels and provided a parts list. The Model 1911 was designed by Thomas C. Johnson. It came to be because John M. Browning and Winchester did not come to terms on what became the Browning self loader and the Remington Model 11. Johnson had to work around patents he had helped Browning acquire. Especially in outward appearance the Model 1911 was like the auto loading rifles which Johnson designed.

The Winchester Self-Loading Shotgun is a recoil operated, hammerless, take down, five shot repeater. The recoil developed by the discharge of the gun cocks the hammer, ejects the fired shell, feeds a loaded shell from the magazine into the chamber and leaves the gun ready to be shot again. As the trigger must be pulled for each shot fired, the gun is at all times as completely under the control of the user as any double or single barreled gun. The loading and shooting of this gun being governed by the trigger finger, it has been aptly called the "Trigger Controlled Repeater." Although wonderful in operation, Winchester Self-Loading Shotgun is neither complicated, cumbersome nor apt to get out of order with any reasonable use. The design and operation of the gun are mechanically correct, and the parts, which are few and strong, are made of the very best materials, and are tested and inspected with great care before being assembled. In shooting quality, grace of outline, balance and in those many other details which go to make up a good gun, this new model keeps pace with the established high Winchester standard.

As in all Winchester guns the element of safety has been carefully and successfully accomplished in designing the Winchester Self-Loading Shotgun. Three separate and distinct features of the construction of this gun make it impossible to discharge it before the action is completely closed and the breech-bolt locked in place. The trigger cannot come in contact with the sear until the breech-bolt is locked in place. The locking block, except when locked in place, positively prevents the firing pin from moving forward. The fall of the hammer is blocked by the locking block operating rod until the breech-bolt is locked in place.

The Winchester Self-Loading Shotgun has all the good points of other recoil operated shotguns, but none of their faults. It also has many distinctive and exclusive features which have led sportsmen to pronounce it the finest and latest example of progress in the art of gun making. Some of the most important of these new ideas and improvements are:—

The barrel, receiver, magazine and all working parts of this gun throughout are made of Nickel steel, which has a far greater tensile strength and elastic limit than the steel used by other makers. The magazine lug and front sight are integral with the barrel, the whole piece being machined from one solid forging. This is a much stronger and more lasting construction than when these parts are made separately and brazed to the barrel.

A gun cannot truthfully be said to boast of a "Bump of Knowledge," but the Winchester Self-Loading Shotgun has a "Bump of Strength," which greatly increases the resistance of the receiver at the point of the greatest strain. In recoil operated shotguns, the strain of the rearward travel of the breech-bolt is greatest on the walls of the receiver where the sides and end join. Although this strain is not as great in the Winchester Self-Loading Shotgun as in other makes, because of its Divided Recoil feature, still the "Bump of Strength," by increasing the thickness of the walls of the receiver at the point of the greatest strain, and supporting it both in front and behind, adds greatly to the strength of the receiver and makes it the safest used on any similar type of gun. . .

The Model 1911 on p. 44 is Plain Finished, or Standard no. 28XX, 12 ga., 26″ barrel.

Instead of the accumulated force of the recoil coming upon the rear and top of the receiver, as in other recoil operated shotguns, the Winchester Self-Loader is so designed that the recoil is divided or broken. The main force of the recoil is absorbed by an elastic buffer located forward of the lower front end of the receiver and the remainder by a similar device which makes a cushion between the rear end of the bolt and the rear end of the receiver. By dividing the recoil in this way the shooter feels it much less than where any other system of absorbing it is employed. This makes the Winchester Self-Loading Shotgun much pleasanter to shoot than any other similar type of gun. We do not make the absurd claim that all recoil is eliminated in this gun, because it is utilized to operate the reloading mechanism, but we do say, without fear of contradiction, that the Winchester Self-Loading Shotgun "kicks" less than any other recoil operated gun. Another particularly desirable feature of the Divided Recoil is the minimizing of the "whip" or "jump" of the muzzle of the gun when shooting. This is due to the fact that the recoil of the Winchester Self-Loader expends its force lower vertically, nearer the horizontal center of the gun and in more direct line with the shooter's shoulder, instead of at the top and rear of the receiver, as is the case in other similar guns. This absence of "jump" or "whip" of the muzzle makes it much easier to shoot the second shot accurately with a Winchester Self-Loader than with any other recoil operated shotgun.

The Winchester Self-Loading Shotgun will operate with complete certainty and safety with any properly loaded paper shell, from a "blank" to the maximum 12 gauge loads, either smokeless or black powder, loaded by this company, without the slightest change or readjustment. It requires no extra oiling to make it work with light loads nor the use of any additional parts to have it operate with heavy loads. It is a gun that requires no favoring. As it is often desirable to shift instantly from a heavy to a light load, sportsmen will welcome a recoil operated shotgun with which this can be done without tinkering with the mechanism.

The two part take-down system used in this gun is simple, strong, and handy. By turning the take-down screw at the rear of the receiver a few times the gun separates into two parts, the stock and guard being in one, and the barrel, magazine and receiver in the other. When taken down, the working parts of the action are accessible for cleaning. In taking down the Winchester Self-Loader, there are no parts separated from the guard, barrel or magazine, to be left behind or lost.

There are no moving parts outside of the receiver to catch in the clothing, or any projections or sharp points to injure the hands of the user of a Winchester Self-Loading Shotgun. The bolt catch is located at the rear of the receiver where it is handy to reach without the user running any risk of having his fingers caught by the bolt as it moves forward. The receiver is entirely free from pins, screws or assembling holes to weaken it. In recoil operated firearms the jar will shake loose receiver pins and screws almost invariably. This defect, common to this type of arms, has been overcome by the Winchester patented system of construction.

The trigger lock on this gun operates crosswise, which makes it impossible to be jarred out of place by the recoil. It is conveniently located in the guard so that it can be readily operated by the trigger finger. The position of the lock can be quickly told by sight or feeling. When the lock is off and the trigger can be pulled, the lock shows a red band of warning.

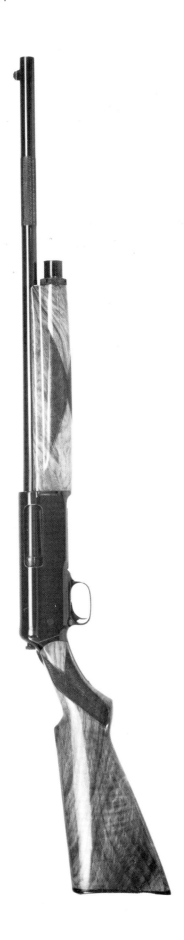

By simply pressing in the bolt catch, the breech-bolt will be locked back and the gun remain open after the next shot is fired. This is a marked advantage over other recoil operated firearms, which only remain open when there are no more shells in the magazine. Locking the bolt so that the gun will remain open at the option of the shooter, facilitates its use as a single loader, the changing of a shell or cleaning of the barrel, etc.

Filling the magazine is not complicated by the necessity of pressing any carrier release. To throw the first shell into the chamber, the barrel is employed very much as it is in the loading of a double barreled gun. Instead of tipping down the barrel, it is drawn rearward as far as it will go. A band is knurled around the barrel, which affords a good grip, no matter what the condition of the hands or barrel may be.

The trigger pull is short, smooth and light. An aperture in the forward end of the bolt makes it possible to see readily without opening the breech whether or not there is a loaded shell in the chamber. If there is any shell in the chamber, it must of necessity be a loaded one, for a shell as soon as it is fired in the gun is ejected by its own recoil.

The releasing of the breech-bolt is not dependent upon a shell's emerging from the magazine. The bolt acts independently of the shell, thus assuring much greater reliability of the gun as a repeater.

The extraction and ejection of the fired shells are absolutely positive in this gun.

All springs used in this gun are made of special high tension wire, which makes them much more durable than ordinary flat springs.

The front sight can be caught by the eye quickly and easily, as a bright point of tin is fused to the steel base. This construction prevents the sight tip from being jarred off.

On all orders for Winchester Self-Loading Shotguns we will send guns made according to the following specifications, unless instructed to the contrary:—

Barrel: Full choke, 26 inch Nickel steel, chambered for 2¾ inch shells. Modified choke or cylinder bore barrels or barrels 28 inches long will be furnished without extra charge. Matted barrels will be furnished at the usual increased charge for this extra. Stock: Pistol grip, handsomely finished wood, 13¾ inches long with 1⅝ inches drop at comb and 2⅜ inches drop at heel. Butt Plate: Rubber. Fancy walnut or plain wood handmade stocks of special lengths or drops, straight or pistol grip, will be furnished at the regular increased charge for such extras. Receiver: Blued and matted on top along the line of sight.

Interchangeable 26 or 28 inch Nickel steel barrels, full or modified choke or cylinder bore, can be furnished. Extra barrel complete with magazine, forearm, etc., $20.00. In all cases, extra barrels will have to be fitted at our armory. . .

PRICE LIST OF MODEL 1911 SELF-LOADING SHOTGUN

Standard Gun, 12 Gauge, 26 inch Nickel Steel Barrel, Pistol Grip Stock of plain wood. Weight about 7¾ pounds,	$38.00
Fancy Walnut Stock and Forearm,	13.00
Checking Stock and Forearm,	5.00
Extra Length or Drop of Stock to order	10.00
Matting Barrel,	5.00
Interchangeable Barrel with Magazine and Forearm complete,	20.00

Fancy Finished Model 1911, 12 ga., 28″. Courtesy of the Winchester Museum, Buffalo Bill Historical Center, Cody, Wyoming.

Plain Finished or Standard Gun 1911–1926

The plain finished grade was supplied with the features of the standard gun listed above. Butt stocks were laminated of three pieces of birch. The forearm was birch with a rock elm insert.

Fancy Finished 1911–1918

The fancy finished grade was first listed at $56.00. It had the same features as the plain finished plus fancy walnut pistol grip stock and forearm, checked.

Trap 1913–1926

The trap grade had a matted barrel and selected fancy handmade, oil-finished stock with straight or pistol grip, checked, and checked rubber butt plate. Straight grip stocks were standard. Pistol grip stocks were supplied at no extra charge. The forearm was fancy and checked. Stocks could be ordered to dimension within limits. This gun was first listed at $70.00.

Pigeon 1913–1926

The pigeon grade, first listed at $150.00, was the same as the trap grade with elaborate engraving on the receiver. Catalogs showed a duck scene on the right side.

The higher grades were last shown in the 1918 catalog. The 1920 catalog listed only the standard gun, but price lists through 1926 showed higher grades. The March 1, 1926 price list showed the standard gun at $72.90, the trap at $120.20, and the pigeon at $234.80. Catalog no. 83 was used from 1925 to 1929 with price lists loose inserted and special notes about changes in the line glued in as page 1. Evidently, some of each of these three grades remained in stock when the gun was discontinued in 1925. Approximately 82,774 were made, and some were assembled as late as 1928.

Special Notes

1. The sight on the Model 1911 had a "non-tarnishing alloyed tip." This was probably German silver.
2. Madis (1980, p. 194–195) cited a designer as having said that 55 changes were made during the first three years of production. Some changes are known. After 4300, an "A" appeared after serial numbers to denote some of the changes. Intermittently after perhaps 5200, the magazine cap was knurled and 3/32 inch longer than the previous one. Later caps had a larger flare where they met the fore end. The model designation was changed to 11 in 1918. Grade designations were not engraved on bolts as on the 1897.
3. Although the Model 11 sold in acceptable quantities it acquired a bad reputation. People accustomed to doubles and slide actions, or Browning and similar autoloaders did not adapt well to opening the gun via the knurled section of the barrel. I know two persons who shot off a middle finger because they opened up the action by pulling on the end of the barrel instead of the knurled section. Granted, they were holding the trigger as they operated the action, but

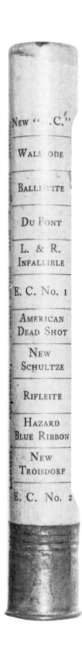

Leader brass shell heads were used to make up powder samples. This specimen made ca 1898 is among the four variations known.

there were safer guns. It is true that heavy use wore the friction points to such an extent that recoil became excessive. It is rumored that the gun broke when used with heavy loads. The greatest problem with the plain finished (standard) guns was cracked forearms and stocks with the laminations coming apart, probably because stock glue was not waterproof. Some are found with Model 40 forearms adapted to them. Nearly all recoil operated auto loaders were hard on wood, but the Model 11 was probably the worst.

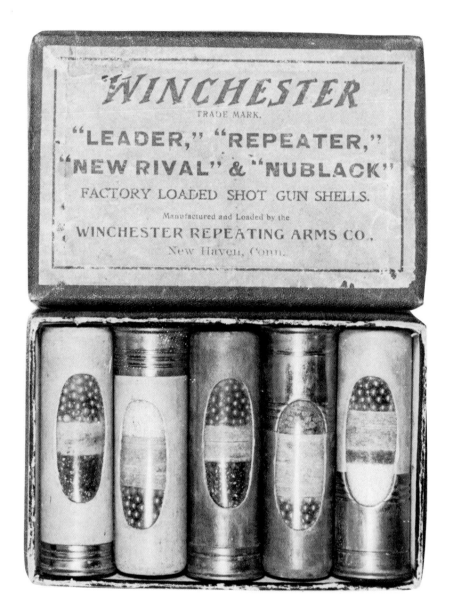

Boxed window shells illustrate which shells were offered at the same time. This one was produced ca 1905.

WINCHESTER SHOTSHELL SAMPLES

Sample display cases were an important part of the arms and ammunition sales-man's materials. The case on the following pages can be closely dated because the STAR shells are included. The October 1893 catalog lists Winchester STAR shells and catalog no. 52, April 1894 does not. Evidently, the display was made up in late 1893 or early 1894.

Winchester first offered shotshells in 1877 and until 1894 listed no more than two kinds of brass shells and four kinds of paper shells at a time. Most of the time only two or three kinds of paper shells were offered. Sample cases may have been made up earlier, but they would have been much smaller unless they included all gauges. This may be the most elaborate salesman's sample of Winchester's shotshell com-ponents ever produced. Like cartridge board shells, the specimens in this case are held in with a wire. However, the wire enters the mouth of the shell and does not pierce the case wall.

Specifications

Dimensions: $12^{11}/_{16} \times 6^{9}/_{16}''$ and $2\frac{3}{4}''$ deep.

Closure—a single brass hook and eye.

Cover—pebble grained dark gray cloth over wood.

Interior—paper lining, probably originally purple but faded to a metallic deep blue, lettering in gold.

Shotshell inventory, beginning at 9 o'clock and working clockwise.

—WINCHESTER No 16, $2^{9}/_{16}''$, dark gray case.
—WINCHESTER No 14, $2^{9}/_{16}''$, dark gray.
—WINCHESTER No 12, $2\frac{5}{8}''$, metal lined, dark gray.
—W.R.A.Co No 12 RIVAL, $2\frac{5}{8}''$, brown case.
—W.R.A.Co No 10 RIVAL, $2\frac{7}{8}''$, brown.
—WINCHESTER No 12 LEADER, $2\frac{5}{8}''$, red case.
—WINCHESTER No 12 BLUE RIVAL, $2\frac{5}{8}''$, dark blue case.
—WINCHESTER No 10 BLUE RIVAL, $2\frac{7}{8}''$, dark blue.
—W.R.A.Co No 12 STAR, $2\frac{3}{4}''$, dark gray to black.
—W.R.A.Co No 10 STAR, $2\frac{7}{8}''$, dark gray.
—WINCHESTER No 10, $2\frac{5}{8}''$, brass.
—WINCHESTER No 14, $2\frac{3}{8}''$, brass.
—WINCHESTER No 16, $2\frac{1}{2}''$, brass
—W.R.A.Co No 12 RIVAL, $2\frac{5}{8}''$, brass.
—WINCHESTER No 8, $3''$, brass.
—WINCHESTER No 20, $2\frac{1}{2}''$, brass.

(First illustrated in the *International Cartridge Collector*, Issue 317, July–August 1983)

100 WINCHESTER 28 GA.

Trade Marks Reg. U. S. Pat. Off. and Throughout the World

REPEATER

GRADE

1910 EMPTY

WATER-PROOFED

PAPER SHOT SHELLS

PRIMED WITH THE

WINCHESTER NEW No. 4 PRIMER

Manufactured by the

WINCHESTER REPEATING ARMS CO.

NEW HAVEN, CONN., U. S. A.

This is the most unusual Repeater 100's box. 1910 was printed instead of 1901. Some have a stick-on correction. Repeater primed empties were popular for four decades. Gauges, years of introduction and years of discontinuance were: 10 and 12, 1896–1937; 14, 1897–1921; 16 and 20, 1896–1937; 24, 1904–1927; 28, 1904–1937; 32, and 410 2″ and 410 2½″, 1920–1937; 410 3″, 1936–1937. Most Repeater shells were yellow. The box is cream with brown lettering.

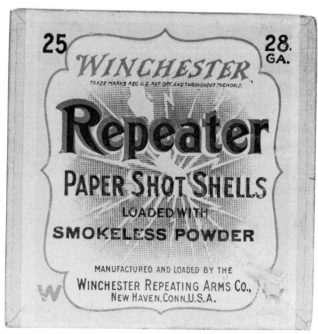

This was the first style Repeater box for loaded shells. Gauges, years of introduction and years of discontinuance of Repeater shells were: 10, 12, 16, and 20, 1900–1938; 24, 1905–1921; 28, 1905–1938; 32, 1916–1925; 410 2″, 1916–1927; 410 2½″, 1923–1927. The label is blue and red on cream. The next box at right was much more attractive, with yellow on white and red and blue print.

Repeater Brush loads were very popular. Gauges, years of introduction, and years of discontinuance were: 12 and 16, 1905–1938; 20, 1913–1938. The label on the box below is yellow on white with red and blue print.

The first Repeater Staynless shells were not speed loads. It was the new primer that was stainless. The label is blue with red and white print.

Repeater Speed Loads were introduced in 1927 in 10, 12, 16 and 20 gauges, and .410 2″ and .410 2½″. The .410 2″ shells were discontinued in 1930 and the rest were dropped in 1932. Most Speed Load shells were red. The label is blue with white and red print.

This box was introduced sometime before 1932, when it was discontinued. It has red and blue print on the white label. The shell it contained was the same type illustrated lower left on p. 52. Red-case Speed Load shells, so headstamped (specimen at right), were introduced in 1932 in 10, 12, 16 and 20 gauges, and .410 2½ but remained in production only until 1933.

Repeater Super Speed shells were reintroduced in 1933. Note the print on the case wall and the battery cup primer. These shells, also red, were discontinued in 1937.

From left—Plain Finished 12 ga., 30″. This is an early gun with half pistol grip, small corrugated forearm, and no groove in the receiver top.

Riot Gun, no. 1739XXX, 12 ga., 20″. Illinois State Police gun, so marked on right side of buttstock.

Chapter 7

MODEL 1912/12

Among shotguns only the Model 12 rivals the Model 94 for being synonymous with the name "Winchester." The first Model 1912's were delivered to the warehouse on August 30, 1912. The back of catalog no. 78, January 1913, introduced the Model 1912 hammerless 20 gauge repeating shotgun with nickel steel construction as "The Lightest, Strongest, and Handsomest Repeating Shotgun Made" at $30.00 list. The prose beginning on page 132 of this catalog was even more verbose.

The increasing demand for the smaller gauge shotguns has raised a call for a really first-class, correctly-proportioned, small-gauge repeater. In answer to this call the Winchester Model 1912, 20 gauge, Hammerless Repeating Shotgun is offered, with the confidence that it will receive the indorsement of sportsmen in general and make a strong appeal to the practical sense of the occasional user of the shotgun, as well as to his conception of balance, proportion, and beauty. When the excellent work of the 20 gauge gun is considered, together with the advantage of its light weight and recoil, it is safe to predict that a wide use of it will ensue. With the advent of this superb new repeater, we look for new records for the small gauge and an increase in the popularity of trap shooting and gunning in the field, as none can now complain of weight or recoil.

As the illustration shows, the new Winchester Hammerless Repeating Shotgun is the epitome of grace and symmetry from butt to muzzle. In graceful curve and refinement of detail and finish, no other repeater approaches it. There is not a screw or pin to be seen to mar its beauty, collect rust and dirt, or work loose; nor any projection or moving part to catch in brush and clothing or injure the hands. The finely proportioned stock has the popular full comb, and a small well-rounded grip, which fits the hand comfortably and joins the receiver in a graceful flowing line. The receiver is matted along the line of sight. The action slide handle is the best ever designed. It tapers slightly forward with a gentle curve, and fits nicely and comfortably in the hand. Its shape and length set off to advantage the beautiful lines of the gun. The length of the gun over all is 43½ inches, and the dimensions of the stock are as follows: Length, 13⅝ inches; Drop at Comb, 1⁷⁄₁₆ inches, Drop at Heel, 2⁷⁄₁₆ inches. The weight of the gun is about 5¾ pounds, which makes it by far the lightest repeating shotgun on the market. It is chambered for 2½ inch shells, and is a 20 gauge gun in every respect: not a large gauge gun with a small gauge barrel.

All the metal parts of this gun are made of Nickel steel, which has about double the breaking strength of ordinary steel, such as is used in repeating shotguns of other makes; and all springs are made of high tension spring wire, which is not liable to break or take on a permanent set from use. This construction insures a gun of great strength and durability.

The receiver of this gun is made of solid Nickel steel, closed at the rear. No safer construction could be devised.

No noticeable effort is required to operate this gun. The action works with an ease and smoothness unknown in any other system. The shells are loaded into the magazine through the bottom of the receiver, one shell after another being pressed against the carrier and forward into the magazine. The action is then operated, first pressing upward the action slide lock, then drawing the action

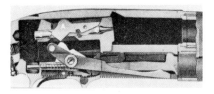

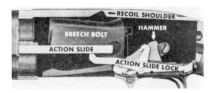

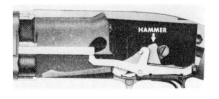

Catalog cross-section drawings showing Model 12 safety features. No. 1.
(a) Retractor
(b) Hammer
(c) Firing Pin

No. 2. Hammer is locked out of trigger's control by action slide lock during entire reloading operation.

No. 3. Action here is all but closed. Hammer still locked back and sear notch of hammer mechanically separated from sear.

Trench Gun no. 996XXX, 12 ga., 20″.

slide handle backward and forward. This cocks the gun, throws a loaded shell into the chamber, and prepares the gun for firing. It is not necessary to manually release the action slide lock after firing, as the recoil does this automatically. The loaded shells can be removed from the magazine, without working them through the action, by pressing up the carrier, and allowing them to be forced out by the magazine spring. By pressing up the action slide lock and drawing back the action slide handle, a loaded shell can be removed from the chamber, without firing, while the gun is cocked.

This gun can be separated into two parts quickly and easily, the stock and action remaining in one part and the barrel and magazine in the other. No tools are required and no small parts are released to be lost. The two parts are locked together by the simple interrupted screw system, which has been so successfully used on the Winchester Model 1897 "Take Down" Repeating Shotgun. The action slide and handle are held forward by friction, so that in putting the gun together, attention to this detail is not demanded. When the gun is taken apart, the barrel may be cleaned from either end.

The trigger lock on this gun is of the cross bolt type and cannot be jarred out of place by the recoil. Located in the guard, it may be readily operated by the trigger finger. Its position can be easily determined by sight or feeling.

It is well known that for shooting qualities, Winchester guns have no superior. The new 20 gauge gun fully maintains the Winchester standard for strong and accurate shooting. It is bored to shoot smokeless powder, and in full choke bore will pattern at least 65% of the shot charge in a 30-inch circle at 40 yards. As the barrel is made of Nickel steel, it combines maximum strength with minimum weight. It may be fitted with a matted rib, if desired.

Interchangeable Nickel steel barrels, full or modified choke, or cylinder bore, can be furnished for this gun. List price of interchangeable barrel complete with magazine, action slide handle, etc., $16.50. In all cases, extra barrels will have to be fitted at our armory.

PRICE LIST OF MODEL 1912, 20 GAUGE SHOTGUN.

Standard Gun, 20 Gauge, 25 inch Nickel Steel Barrel, chambered for 2½ inch Shells, Plain Walnut Pistol Grip Stock and Action Slide Handle, Length of Stock 13⅝ inches, Drop at Comb, 1⁷⁄₁₆ inches, Drop at Heel, 2⁷⁄₁₆ inches, Rubber Butt Plate, Weight about 5¾ pounds, 6 shots — $30.00

Fancy Walut Stock and Action Slide Handle, not checked — 13.00
Checking Fancy Stock and Action Slide Handle — 5.00
Extra Length or Drop of Stock to order — 10.00
Matted Rib — 5.00
Interchangeable Barrel, Nickel Steel, complete with Magazine and Action Slide Handle — 16.50

Because they are a critical lot, serious collectors abhor untrammeled advertising. But, most would not challenge use of superlatives for the Model 12. It was a major departure from previous designs, was much emulated, and lasted far longer than most models of any make. That 100,000 were sold during the first few years attested to the efficacy of the gun and its advertising.

It is important to understand who designed the 1912. During 1902, John M. Browning and T. G. Bennett of Winchester broke negotiations concerning what came to be the Browning and Remington Model 11 auto loading shotguns. Thomas Crossley Johnson, a Winchester inventor, designed the Model 1911, the Model 1912, the Thumb Trigger, and the Models 1903, 1904, 1905, 1907, and 1910 self-loading rifles. Some of these utilized minor features of models previously designed by Browning. It is easy to see that the take-down feature on the Model 1912 was the same as on the 1897. This was not a Browning contribution. The patent Model 1897 was a solid frame.

The slide actions Browning designed during this period were the grotesque Model 520 Stevens (1903–1904) and the rather gracious Model 17 Remington (1921), which outlasted the Model 12 as the Ithaca Model 37.

During the first year or so, the 1912 was available only in 20 gauge and in plain and fancy finished grades.

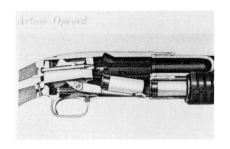

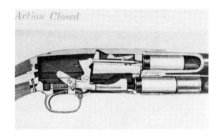

Plain Finished, Standard or Field 1913–1963

The standard gun was offered in several variations in addition to the standard barrel lengths and chokes. The riot gun was introduced in 1918 and discontinued in 1963. Catalogs listed riot and trench guns in 12 gauge only. Some, perhaps ten, riot guns were made up in 16 gauge for a Tennessee prison. They were sold to prison personnel in 1955 and are among the rarest of Winchesters. The trench gun was introduced in 1918 and was made on special order only after WW I. The heavy duck gun was introduced in 1935 and discontinued in 1963. (It was also made in other than standard grades as explained below.) The 28 gauge was introduced in 1937, chambered for 2⅞ inch shells or for 2½ inch shells on special order in 26 inch and 28 inch with full, modified or cylinder bore and in 26 or 28 inch solid matted rib with full or modified bore. The wood on standard guns underwent several changes. Three corrugated slide handles were used. The first was only as long and as large in diameter as the slide handle metal. The second or semi beavertail was the same length but larger in diameter with a flat bottom. The third or beavertail was full round and extended to the rear—but not as much as extension slide handles. Corresponding buttstocks went from half to full pistol grips and were successively straighter and longer, excepting that the stock for the Heavy Duck Gun was once shortened. For a time after 1954, field guns could be special ordered with Winchester Special Ventilated Ribs.

Fancy Finished 1913, 20 Gauge

Fancy finished meant "fancy walnut pistol grip stock and forearm checked." Catalog no. 79,1914, greatly expanded the offering. It listed plain finished or standard guns in 12, 16 and 20 gauge. These had 2¾, 2⁹⁄₁₆, and 2½ inch chambers. (From 1930 on, all 12, 16, and 20 gauge chambers were 2¾.) The 16 gauge was made on the 20 gauge action as was the 28 gauge.

Tournament Gun 1914–1931, 12 Gauge

The 1914 catalog introduced the tournament gun. This was a ready-made gun for trap shooting. It had a raised matted rib (no center bead) straight grip (no black diamonds), checked stock and forearm, and oil finish which was standard on high grade guns for a long time. This grade was discontinued on July 2, 1931 and was succeeded by the Standard Trap.

Tournament, trap, and pigeon guns could be had with Winchester ventilated ribs and extension slide handles after 1919. Catalog no. 82 and subsequent ones showed slide handles on 12 gauge guns much larger than the post WW II ones. Some guns which were fitted with these slide handles had pistol grips shaped almost like what one would expect on a piece with a schnabel forearm. The first

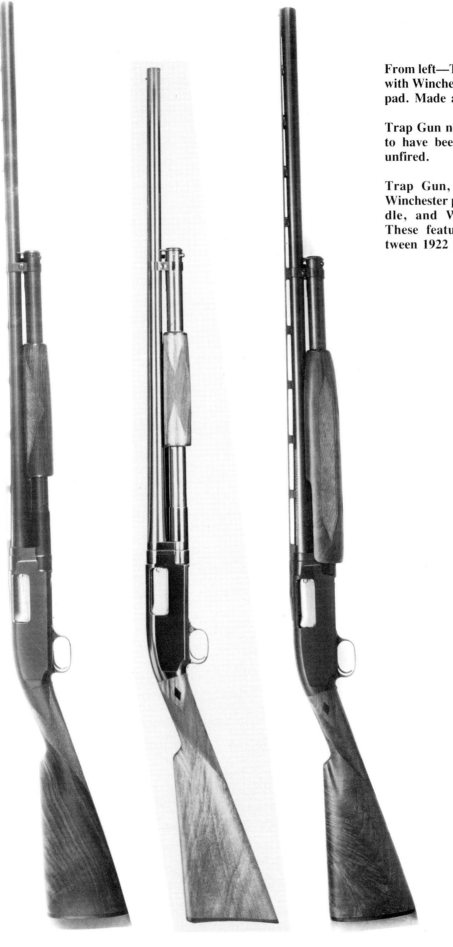

From left—Tournament Gun, 12 ga., 30″, with Winchester Ventilated Rib and recoil pad. Made after 1922.

Trap Gun no. 109XXX, 20 ga., 25″. Said to have been made in 1917, it remains unfired.

Trap Gun, 12 ga., 30″. Straight grip, Winchester pad, large extension slide handle, and Winchester Ventilated Rib. These features mean manufacture between 1922 and 1931.

pistol grips pictured in catalogs did not have caps. Catalog no. 82 also showed a recoil pad which was probably a Hawkins. The Winchester solid red pad was patented in 1922 and first appeared in catalog no. 83.

Trap Gun 1914–1931: 12, 16, and 20 Gauge

Introduced in catalog no. 82, this gun was made to order. Stocks on this grade were selected fancy walnut, were checked, had oil finish and black diamonds, and were made to customer specifications without extra charge. Standard dimensions were also furnished. Matted barrels (not matted ribs) were furnished without extra charge. The trap gun was discontinued on July 2, 1931 and was succeeded by the Special Trap.

Pigeon Gun 1914–1941: 12, 16, and 20 Gauge

This gun was "beautifully and elaborately engraved, and finished with especial care . . . to the same specifications and with the same options as the 'Trap' gun, except the length of barrel is 28 instead of 30 inches." Barrels on 16 gauge guns were 26 inches long and barrels on 20 gauge guns were 25 inches long—the standard lengths for this period. The 25 inch 20 gauge was discontinued in 1935. The right side of the receiver had an English setter and an English pointer and quail. The older guns had more elaborate scrolls. The later guns were very much like the later number 5 engraving. The catalog pictures showed scrolls on the receiver top. Of course, receiver tops were not engraved after sandblasted finish became standard on trap and skeet receiver tops. Early pigeon engraving was varied to suit customer tastes. The 28 gauge was introduced in 1937 and was supplied in either field or skeet length/choke combinations.

Standard Trap Grade 1930–1939: 12, 16, and 20 Gauge

This grade was available with straight or pistol grip (no black diamonds). The early pistol grip had no cap. The solid, red pad was standard. A semi-beavertail slide handle no longer than the slide handle metal could be had on this grade, on the Special Trap, and on the Pigeon at no extra charge. "STANDARD TRAP" was stamped on the receiver extension in block letters. It should be stressed that during this period "trap" was still a grade and was not for trap shooting only. Beginning in 1933, skeet 1 and 2 chokes were available. (The skeet chokes were first offered in Model 21's.) The 28 gauge was introduced in 1937 in field and skeet length/choke combinations.

Special Trap Grade 1930–1939: 12, 16, and 20 Gauge

This was a special order gun with straight or pistol grip, black diamonds, rubber butt plate, and the large extension slide handle. Black diamonds were discontinued in 1939, though remaining stocks were used. Noshoc, Hawkins, several Jostom, D-W, and Goodrich pads could be ordered at no extra charge. The 28 gauge was introduced in 1937 and was likely supplied in either field or skeet length/choke combinations.

60

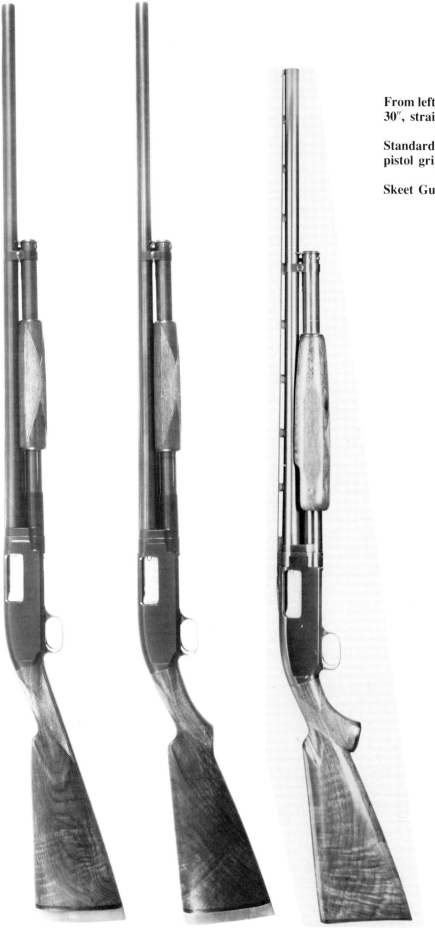

From left—Standard Trap Grade, 12 ga., 30″, straight grip.

Standard Trap grade, 12 ga., 30″, half pistol grip.

Skeet Gun no. 1210XXX, 12 ga., 26¾″.

Skeet Gun 1933–1963

Solid raised matted ribs in 12, 16, and 20 gauge (26-inch barrels) were authorized on November 17, 1933 and appeared in the 1934 catalog. Some catalogs in the middle 1930's called it the Standard Grade Skeet Gun. These had the beavertail slide handle which appeared to the end of production, and full pistol grips. Skeet guns with plain barrels were authorized on January 20, 1937 and were last listed in 1947, the Cutts Compensator was authorized on August 4,1938 in 12 and on February 8, 1939 in 16 and 20 gauge. The post-war catalogs showed the plain barrel 12 gauge skeet gun with integral flange for the Cutts Compensator through January 24, 1955. The December 30, 1955 catalog did not. During the middle 1950s at least, Winchester offered to fit the popular choke devices on any single barrel repeater. Some were installed on barrels with no choke markings. Starting sometime in the 1950s and until 1955 Cutts Compensators were an option on 20 and 28 gauge skeet guns. It is hard to tell which were factory installed and which were not, unless you have the box.

The 28 gauge solid rib skeet was introduced in 1937 with 26 inch barrel. Advanced collectors believe that both 26 and 28 inch barrels were available.

The Winchester ventilated rib 12 gauge 26¾-inch barrel gun was introduced in 1937 and discontinued in 1955. The December 30, 1955 catalog showed skeet guns with only 26 inch Winchester Special Ventilated Rib barrels in 12, 20, and 28 inch gauge. This marked the end of solid rib skeet guns. Many skeet guns had "SKEET" stamped near serial numbers. From 1961 to 1963, 12 and 20 gauge skeet guns and all trap guns were made with the New Winchester Ventilated Rib. Several 20 gauge guns with this rib have been examined. Because the 28 gauge was discontinued in 1960, catalogs did not list 28 gauge guns with this rib and it is generally accepted among collectors that none exist.

Heavy Duck Gun 1935–1963, 12 Gauge 3″

This was not a grade, but it deserves separate treatment. The magnum was authorized on February 15, 1935 and discontinued in 1963. The 1936 catalog listed it in Standard Grade, Standard Trap, Special Trap, or Pigeon Grade. The 1939 catalog reduced this to Standard, Trap or Pigeon. Plain and matted rib 30 and 32 inch barrels were available. The 32 inch was discontinued in 1948 or 1949. I have examined a solid rib 30 inch gun with "MODEL 12 TRAP" on the receiver extension, a number of solid rib 30 inch pigeons, several Winchester Special Ventilated Rib 30 inch pigeons, and several standard grade guns with Winchester Special Ventilated ribs. All Winchester Special Ventilated Rib magnum guns examined have sandblasted receiver tops. No magums were fitted with "duck bill" ribs. The 1960 wholesale-retail catalog listed 30 inch solid rib pigeon magnums. This was likely the last mention of solid ribs in Winchester literature.

Trap Gun (New Style) 1938–1963, 12 Gauge

This style was authorized on July 21, 1938. It was very much like the early Standard Trap. New style trap guns did not have black diamonds. (A few are found with black diamonds because remaining Standard Trap stocks were used.) It is likely that because the Special Trap was discontinued, the word standard was simply dropped from the cheaper gun. Early guns had "MODEL 12 TRAP" stamped on the receiver extension. For a time, either the solid or ventilated rib

62

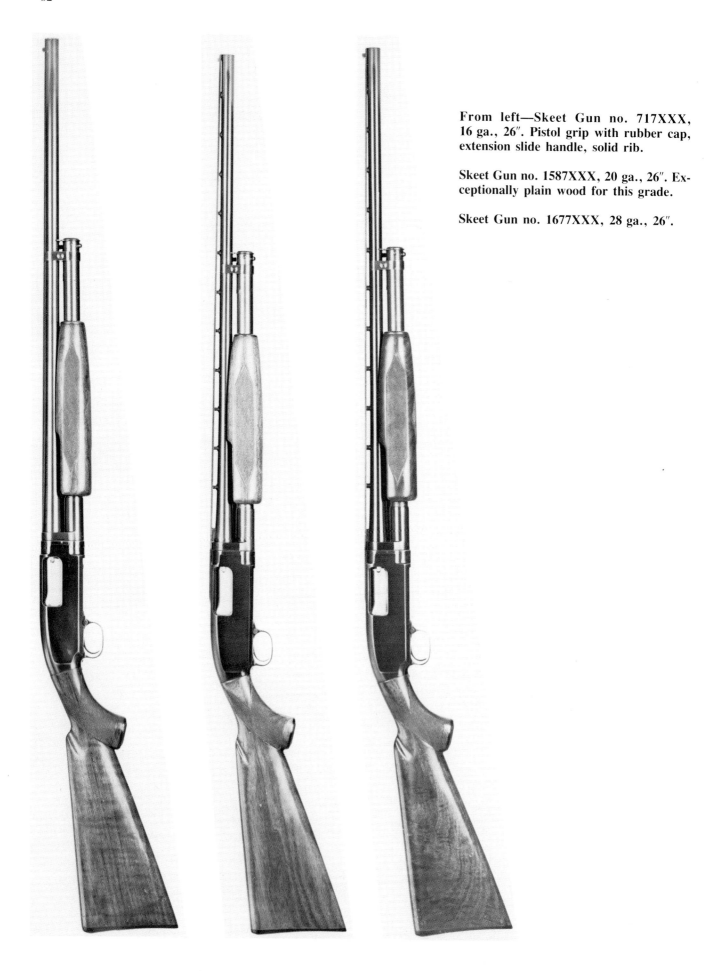

From left—Skeet Gun no. 717XXX, 16 ga., 26″. Pistol grip with rubber cap, extension slide handle, solid rib.

Skeet Gun no. 1587XXX, 20 ga., 26″. Exceptionally plain wood for this grade.

Skeet Gun no. 1677XXX, 28 ga., 26″.

guns could be had with straight or pistol grips. Later, straight grip stocks cost extra. Monte Carlo trap stocks were authorized on December 18, 1940.

Trap Gun, Ladies and Junior Model 1939–1941:
12, 16, 20 Gauge

This gun was authorized in 20 gauge on October 22, 1939 and discontinued on December 31, 1941. The 1940 Wholesale and Retail Price List listed this gun in 28-inch 12 gauge with pistol or straight grip and matted rib, "16 and 20 gauges furnished under same specifications on special order only." Unlike the earlier guns which were marked "Standard Trap" on the receiver extension, Ladies and Junior guns were probably marked "MODEL 12 TRAP." The distinguishing features of this gun were (a) 13 inch pull over, (b) a solid recoil pad of "specially shaped sponge rubber, 2 ply." Otherwise, it was nothing new—just a gun advertised for a special purpose. It is likely the rarest Model 12, especially in 16 and 20 gauge.

New Pigeon Grade, ca 1940

The 1938 catalog showed the same gun which had been depicted for many years with straight stock and black diamonds, the extension slide handle, and the old engraving. Monte Carlo stocks were available at no extra charge. "Special designs, monograms, initials, game scenes, inlay work in silver, gold, or platinum will be executed to order." The 1939 catalog showed a pistol grip gun with black diamonds and the newer number five engraving. The statement about special designs was included.

The next catalog (undated but pre-war) showed the same gun but said, ". . . now furnished in three standard styles . . . and can also be furnished with any style of ornamentation. . . The three standard styles include Pigeon Grade gun without engraving, gun with engraved receiver, and gun with receiver, barrel and trigger guard engraved, both styles of engraving to conform to standard design."

This gun was discontinued in 1941.

Post-War Pigeon Grade 1948–1963

Virtually the same gun was re-introduced in 1948 without engraving, but it could be ordered with any of the standard engraving and carving patterns.

Super Grade Field Gun 1955–1958: 12, 16, 20 Gauge

This gun had a checked stock with rubber pistol grip cap, extension slide handle and matted rib, bored full, modified, or improved cylinder. It was last listed in 1958 and is little known. Many are incorrectly advertised as skeet guns and it is likely that some of the 12 gauge 30 inch guns have been customized into so-called trap guns.

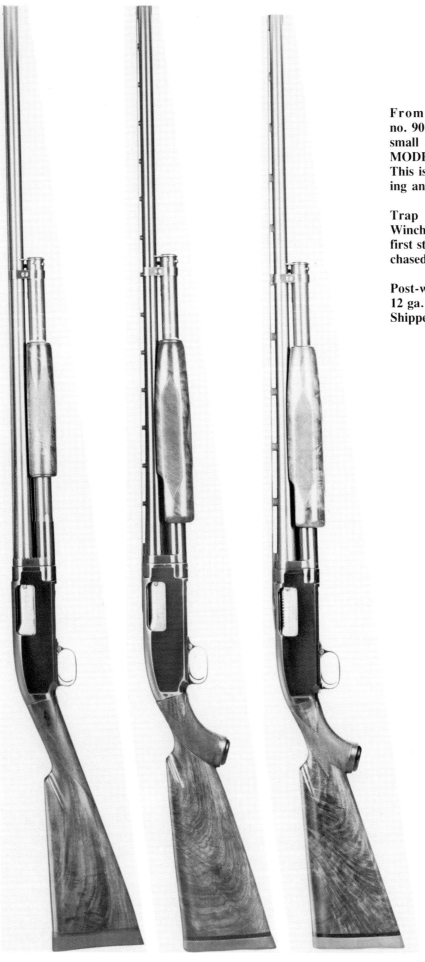

From left—Trap Gun (New Style) no. 901XXX, 12 ga., 30″. Straight grip, small checked forearm and matted rib, MODEL 12 TRAP on receiver extension. This is a transition piece with this marking and black diamonds.

Trap Gun no. 1742XXX, 12 ga., 30″. Winchester Special Ventilated Rib and first steel grip cap. See Appendix B. Purchased new in 1957.

Post-war Pigeon Grade no. 1757XXX, 12 ga., 30″. Winchester Ventilated Rib. Shipped in October 1957.

Model 12 Featherweight 1959–1962, 12 Gauge

Some collectors treat this as a separate model. It was a field grade gun with standard length/choke combinations and no rib or other embellishment. Featherweights did not have cartridge guides and pivots. The instructions which came with the gun played heavily on similarities to the standard gun.

The outstanding natural pointing qualities, effortless operation, trouble-free performance and time-proven durability which have gained the WINCHESTER Model 12 a world-wide reputation as "The Perfect Repeater" are now built into a "Featherweight" version. This shotgun will be the pride of all game shooters, unequalled for ease of carrying thru the marsh or in the field.

Only the finest of gun steels—WINCHESTER Proof (Chrome Molybdenum) steel—is used in the manufacture of your Model 12 Featherweight. Individual parts are carefully treated to exactly the right hardness for strength and wearing qualities . . . then machined and gauged to strict tolerances, superbly finished and fitted for smoothest operation. The graceful receiver is forged from a single billet of steel and closed at both rear and top for utmost protection. The barrel of the Model 12 Featherweight is noted for its strength, uniformity and consistency of pattern performance. Stock and slide handle are of carefully finished American walnut.

The takedown has been designed to give the shooter the greatest simplicity and speed without the use of tools. The barrel and action are of a length that will store easily and be convenient when placed in a carrying case.

Equally popular, is the ease with which your Model 12 Featherweight is loaded or unloaded and its simple, jam-proof loading system from magazine to chamber. The magazine holds four Super-Seal crimp or rolled crimp type shells. With one round in the chamber, your Model 12 Featherweight is a five-shot repeater.

For maximum protection while reloading, the Model 12 Featherweight has three automatic safety features. (1) When the action is in rearward position, the firing pin is locked in the breech bolt, with point fully withdrawn. (2) At the slightest rearward motion of the slide handle, the hammer is immediately secured until action is again closed. (3) When the gun is fired, recoil disengages the action slide lock and slide bar, permitting the action to be manipulated for reloading. If the hammer should fall on an empty chamber, however, or in case of a misfire, a slight forward push on the slide handle is necessary to disengage bar and slide. This provides vital protection in case of a "hang fire."

The Model 12 Featherweight is made in 12 gauge only, with four combinations of barrel length and choke, satisfactory for all types of field shooting. Whatever your choice, in the field or in the gun rack, this sleek, splendid performing repeater will make you proud to be its owner.

Super Pigeon 1963–1972 and 1976–1979, 12 Gauge

Production models were discontinued in 1963 at approximately 1,962,001. A few were made up from remaining parts. Kodl (1981, p.10) reported that number 1,964,384, a regular production gun, was made in 1965. Five hundred sets of 12 gauge components were stored for the Custom Shop, which assembled and finished Super Pigeon guns. Super Pigeons had new Winchester Ventilated Ribs and 12-1A, 1B, or 1C engraving. Some were made with the more ornate styles, including gold dogs and/or birds. During this period as earlier, pigeon guns (and others for that matter) were made to order with embellishments not described in the catalogs.

Featherweight no. 1824XXF, 12 ga., 30″.

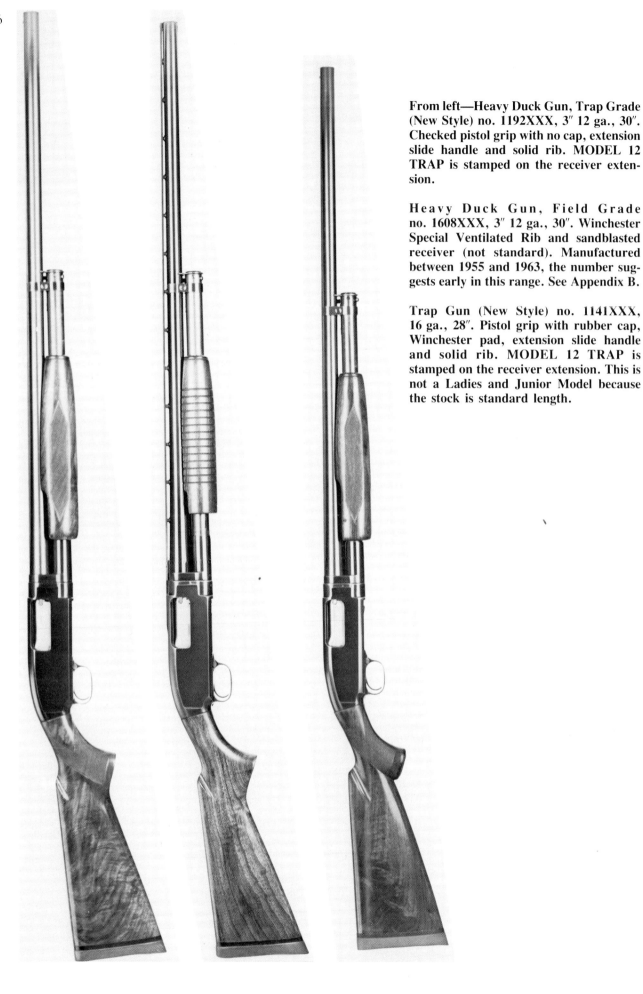

From left—Heavy Duck Gun, Trap Grade (New Style) no. 1192XXX, 3″ 12 ga., 30″. Checked pistol grip with no cap, extension slide handle and solid rib. MODEL 12 TRAP is stamped on the receiver extension.

Heavy Duck Gun, Field Grade no. 1608XXX, 3″ 12 ga., 30″. Winchester Special Ventilated Rib and sandblasted receiver (not standard). Manufactured between 1955 and 1963, the number suggests early in this range. See Appendix B.

Trap Gun (New Style) no. 1141XXX, 16 ga., 28″. Pistol grip with rubber cap, Winchester pad, extension slide handle and solid rib. MODEL 12 TRAP is stamped on the receiver extension. This is not a Ladies and Junior Model because the stock is standard length.

Trap, Skeet and Field 1972–1976, 12 Gauge

Production guns with rectangular post ribs, engine turned bolts and carriers, new checking patterns, and a new metal pistol grip cap saying "Winchester Repeating Arms" were introduced in 1972. Model 12's had been machined from solid steel blanks. New guns were made from investment castings. Receivers, receiver extensions, carriers, bolts, barrel bands, hammers, and guards were castings. By itself, this did not impair quality of the new guns. The prototype trap gun shown at the 1974 Grand American was number 1,990,004. It did not have a "Y" preceding the serial number. Production reached 2,000,000 in 1972. Vice President William Talley presented this gun with a gold medallion to former Secretary of the Treasury John Connally. Talley described the gun and the man as having rugged reliability and long-lived service. The 1973 and 1974 catalogs showed trap, skeet, and field guns; the 1975 catalog showed only trap guns. Production skeet and field guns were discontinued in 1976 and trap guns were discontinued in 1980 at number 2,026,721, the end of a 78-year era.

Ducks Unlimited Commemorative 1975, 12 Gauge

This was a special run for Ducks Unlimited Inc. These guns were numbered from 001 to 800. All had 30 inch, full choke ventilated rib barrels and wood like the last field guns. The left side of the receiver had a bronze medal with engraved canvasback drake and "Ducks Unlimited Commemorative." The right side had a duck in a round vignette like the simplest Super Pigeon. The grip cap had a gold "Ducks Unlimited" insert.

Special Notes

1. The 1918 catalog changed the model designation to Model 12.
2. There were almost no changes in metal parts. Early receivers had no groove, but did have matting approximately one quarter inch wide along the line of sight. Early guns had flat magazine locking pin springs. These were changed to spring wire. Early guns had checking on the protruding part of the action slide lock; later ones were serrated north and south. There were three ejectors: magnum; 12-16-20; and 28 gauge. Near the end of production, the 12-16-20 ejector was supplied on all guns. (This, in part, was why some magnums hung up.) The Y models had some internal differences. The cartridge guide was added in 1938, but it was on again-off again in the post WW II period. Sandblasted receiver tops were authorized for skeet and trap guns on February 10, 1939.
3. There were several ventilated ribs (see page 70). The first and the last were all Winchester. The first, the Winchester Ventilated Rib, is often called the milled rib and was installed only on 12 gauge skeet and higher grade guns. It was called milled because the rib supports were integral parts of the barrel. Material was milled away to leave dovetailed supports for rectangular posts with curved sides. This was a full floating rib. The rib extension on the receiver was shaped like a spoonbill, i.e., one half inch wide at the south end and the same width as the rib where it joined the rib. The top surface of the rib, the rib extension and the receiver from the extension to the butt stock had squiggly lines north and south and east and west. This rib was available from approximately 1919 to 1961 on Tournament, Trap and Pigeon grade guns and from 1937 to 1955 on 12 gauge Skeet guns.

The last rib, the New Winchester Ventilated Rib, was introduced in 1961. It had rectangular posts which were spot welded to the barrel and had dove tailed

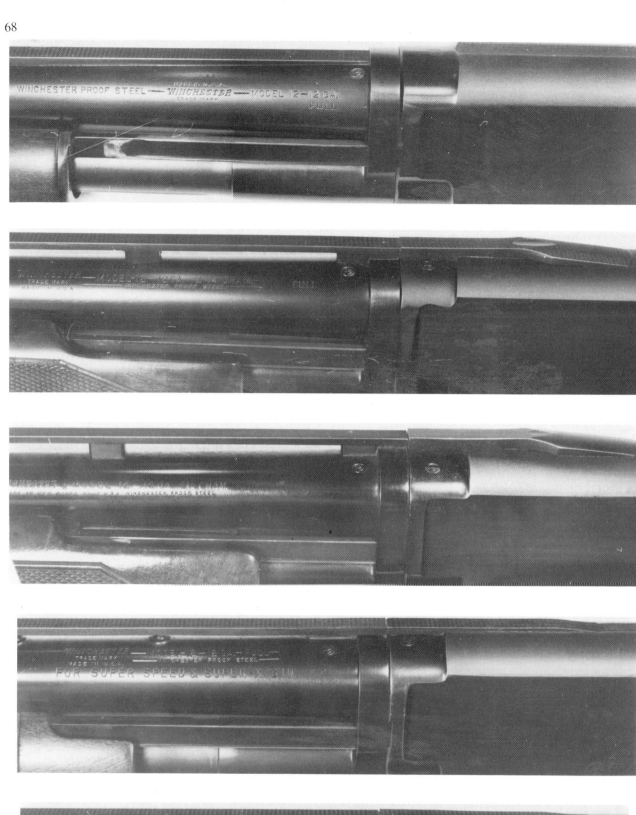

tops. The rib fitted these dove tails and was full floating. The rib extension was shaped like the Winchester Ventilated Rib but it was smooth and the rib had only straight north and south lines. The rib extension and the receiver top were sandblasted. The receiver top had no groove or marks of any kind. This rib appeared on 12 and 20 gauge skeet, trap, and pigeon guns. It was standard on all post-1964 guns (12 gauge only). I have examined three 20 gauge skeet guns with this rib. It is doubtful that it was attached to 28 gauge guns because of year of discontinuance, but I have it from an advanced collector that it was attached to at least one 16 gauge.

For information on the other ribs which appeared on Model 12's we are indebted to Felix A. Bedlan (1981) and Ernie Simmons, Jr. (1982). As they made clear, one must understand rib posts, lines on rib tops, and markings. The *first* Simmons rib was supported by a two-diameter post. This was often called the nail head post. The larger diameter base was brazed to the barrel and the smaller diameter was dovetailed at the top for the rib. According to Bedlan this rib was made for approximately eight years. Appendix B is a Winchester flyer circa 1954, which describes this rib and Model 12 and 42 guns for which it was available as an extra or as an option to the more costly Winchester Ventilated Rib. Note that all target guns including guns with factory installed Cutts Compensators, Magum Duck guns, Pigeon guns, and field guns on special order could be had with this rib. Receivers with this and the second and third varieties may or may not have been sandblasted. I have seen a field magnum with sandblasting and a 42 skeet without sandblasting.

The *second* Simmons rib was supported by a cylindrical, hollow post. Unless the rib is removed these cannot be distinguished from supports for the *third* Simmons rib which had cylindrical but not hollow posts. First, second, and third posts appeared with two types of rib and rib extension tops. Some had squiggly lines north and south and east and west and some had only north and south lines. Because the second and third style posts cannot be distinguished from one another, you can readily find four combinations of posts and tops. The rib extensions were set in a milled slot in the receiver and were secured with a screw from inside the receiver. Receiver tops had the same groove as did field grade guns and were sandblasted. These ribs were installed on 12, 20, and 28 gauge Skeet guns, Trap and Pigeon guns, and magnum guns in field or Pigeon grade.

First, second, and third style Simmons ribs are found with various Simmons trademarks; e.g., "Simmons Gun Specialties, Inc., Kansas City, Mo." or "Simmons Patent." If no Winchester Proof marks show, the gun left the factory as a field grade. If a proof mark shows only on the barrel, the gun left the factory with a solid rib, which Simmons subsequently milled off before installing a ventilated rib.

If no Simmons trademark appears on the rib, it was either installed by Simmons and returned to Winchester in the white or, more likely, was installed by Winchester. Winchester was licensed to install Winchester Special Ventilated Ribs and paid royalties to Simmons Gun Specialties for a number of years. (Ernie

---

From top at left—(1) The raised matted rib or solid rib.

(2) The first Winchester Ventilated Rib, often called the milled rib.

(3) The last or New Winchester Ventilated Rib.

(4) The first Simmons rib.

(5) The second and third Simmons ribs have cylindrical posts. (See pp. 69, 71 and 73 for full details)

TO SECURE YOUR WINCHESTER MODEL 12 SHOTGUN

Fill in specifications of the gun you want on this blank. Keep a copy of it. Turn blank over to your dealer, to ascertain price of the gun as you want it. On your approval he will place your order for your Model 12 in accordance with your exact specifications.

No order will exist until you give your dealer definite instructions to order gun for you.

Stock: ☐ *Pistol Grip* ☐ *Straight* ☐ *Monte Carlo*

Length of Pull (C to C) _____

Drop at Comb (**B to B**) _____

Drop at Heel (**A to A**) _____

Drop at Monte Carlo (E to E) _____

Pitch _____

RECOIL PAD: ☐ *Yes* ☐ *No*

Information on cheekpiece, offset or other special dimensioning: _____

Dealer's Name _____

Dealer's Address _____

12 Gauge Only — Barrel Length _____
Barrel Lengths Available: 26″, 28″, 30″

Choke: _____

SIGHTS: Front   Middle

METAL: ☐   ☐

IVORY BEAD: ☐   ☐

RED BEAD: ☐   ☐

CARVING: ☐ 12A

EXTRA CARVING: ☐ 12B

OPTIONAL: Check One

ENGRAVING: ☐ 12-1A   ☐ 12-1B   ☐ 12-1C

Name _____

Street Number _____

City _____ State _____

Simmons Sr. served as a consultant to Winchester for several years.) A purist would collect only guns without Simmons trademarks because they are all New Haven. But, for a time, Simmons bought Model 12 Skeet, Trap, and Pigeon grade finished guns with plain barrels, installed ribs, and distributed them through its dealers. These are certainly desirable pieces.

The *fourth* Simmons rib had hollow, oval shaped posts. According to Bedlan (1981) it was made from approximately 1957 to 1969 and installed by Simmons for Winchester. Based on examining many model 12's, I can only conclude that the round post ribs were the last ones installed for or by Winchester. All oval shaped posts had ribs with straight north and south lines. None which I have examined had proof marks.

4. Collectors must be careful to avoid guns with other than factory wood or wood from the wrong periods. Initial 12 gauge slide handle metal provided for a 5⁵⁄₁₆″ handle for both plain and higher-grade guns. Sometime between 1916 and 1918 this was changed and slide handles were 6¹¹⁄₁₆″ long. There were six checked slides: (1) the little one with diamond shaped panels on the side on Tournament guns; (2) the little one checked all the way around on Trap and Pigeon guns; (3) the first large extension slide handle; (4) the semi-beavertail no longer than the slide handle metal, which was an option for only a few years; (5) the extension slide handle which was introduced with the skeet guns (checking patterns on this last one were the same for Trap and Skeet guns and slightly smaller on Super Grade Field Guns); and (6) the Pigeon slide handle which had three diamonds on the bottom. (The last production guns had slide handles with checking pattern similar to Pigeon guns.) There were also A and B style slide handles. Some of the very last slide handles used on the 16, 20, and 28 gauge guns were blunt-ended at the rear. Dimensions and shapes of field grade stocks were changed several times. Higher grade stocks were changed much more often. Catalog pictures are the best way to know them.

There were seven grip caps: (1) solid rubber with "Winchester Repeating Arms Co."; (2) steel; (3) steel with depressed oval center and screw showing; (4) same with black aluminum insert with red W; (5) shallow metal with scrolls and no lettering; (6) metal with raised "Winchester Repeating Arms"; (7) same with gold "Ducks Unlimited" insert.

There were two shapes of solid red pads for shotguns. The one used nearly all of the time was only slightly rounded at the edges. The other was longer at the toe. The Ladies and Junior trap gun had a special two-ply pad. A red, bridged pad made by Pachmayr was used for a short period in the 1960's. Finally, there was the rather cheap red bridged pad.

Spotting mis-matches of these features requires a lot of experience. Guns which started life with plain, matted, or matted rib barrels which have Simmons or other ribs are easy to spot. Mis-matched wood is harder to peg. Factory installed muzzle devices and other than Winchester pads should be accepted but are very hard to authenticate. Furthermore, guns which were fitted with new barrels or receivers at the factory or various repair centers may have combination features. For example, there is a solid rib 12 gauge skeet gun with a "Y" preceding the serial number. The receiver had been properly replaced because the recoil shield had been beaten to a knife edge. When the factory no longer had milled rib barrels, barrels with the New Winchester Ventilated Rib were fitted as replacement or extra barrels by the factory or other repair centers. Such oddities should be avoided. Usually their overall condition is also wanting.

5. The January 2, 1930 Retail Price List listed "Stainless Steel Barrels" at $11.75, $29.40, and $35.25 for plain, raised matted rib, and ventilated rib guns. The 1931 catalog listed stainless steel. Subsequent literature did not list the stainless steel option for shotgun barrels.

This is the most ornate Model 12. Engraving no. 1s embraced inlaying, engraving, damascening, and hand carving. The scrolls are arabesque. The light, unbroken lines are gold inlay. Birds are damascened in solid gold and silver, the carving is style As. This specimen is a very early Model 12.

6. Hydro Coil stocks and matching slide handles were available on skeet and trap guns (straight or Monte Carlo) during the last year or so before discontinuance in 1963. They were ivory or walnut colored.

7. To clay target shooters and their gunsmiths, it is obvious that the model 12 will wear faster than many magazine guns. New receiver rings must be fitted before the recoil shield gets hammered because of excess head space. Springs on action slide locks can be troublesome, especially in Y model guns. The other big weakness is the firing pin. Target shooters shoot until the broken pin is beaten so short that they get one or two misfires in a hundred shots. Actually this is a compliment. How many guns can you shoot after the pin breaks? The firing pin retractor wears, too, but it seldom gets so bad that the gun will not shoot. The wear on its top, curved surface is a clear indicator of amount of use. The most common malady is the guard screw. All five external screws should be doped with water glass or a commercial lock tight. A replacement guard screw with a plastic tit cures the matter for people who are compelled to clean the action. Guns which have been fired several hundred thousand times will likely develop other maladies because of excess wear. All of those are easily treated by competent smiths.

The magnum is not a good pumper. The problem is ejection. This can be helped in three ways. (1) The under surface of the breech block can be filed and honed. Removing three to four thousandths makes rear travel easier. (2) The inside of the carrier can be polished to assure that a loaded shell does not bounce up and bump the rim of the fired shell. (3) The tapered or conical surface just to the rear (inside) of the ejection port can be smoothed with emery cloth on a dowel. This makes for less friction on shells as they pivot out the ejection port. Guns with bonafide magnum ejectors, strong carrier springs, and properly shaped extractors will have very few ejection problems, if these modifications are done skillfully. I have it from several men who have killed tens of thousands of geese and ducks with well-tuned Pigeon grade magnums that they have occasional hang-ups—and these are six foot plus, strong men who have used pump guns all their lives.

8. By happenstance the Model 12 with trap wood is extremely well balanced. For the typical trap shooter, it points better than any other trap gun. It is also the least tiring of all trap guns to operate—easier than the Model 31 and 870 Remingtons and all break-open guns. These two advantages, unknown to most trap shooters, are why the Model 12 had resurgences. These were bad for collectors because many good copies were fitted with custom ribs and wood. Because other slide actions are much less expensive to manufacture, and because break-open guns and auto loaders dominate clay target shooting, the Model 12 will likely never be made again. Yet, no one alive today will see the end of Models 12's in the field or on the range. Many will be in regular use as long after 1980 as before.

12-2 *Engraving*

12-3 *Engraving*

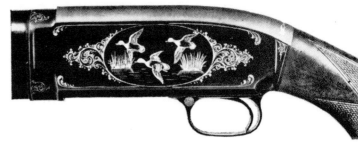

12-4 *Engraving*

12-5 *Engraving*

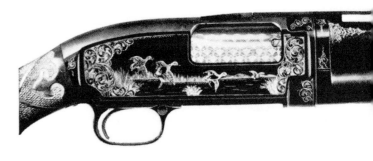

12-A

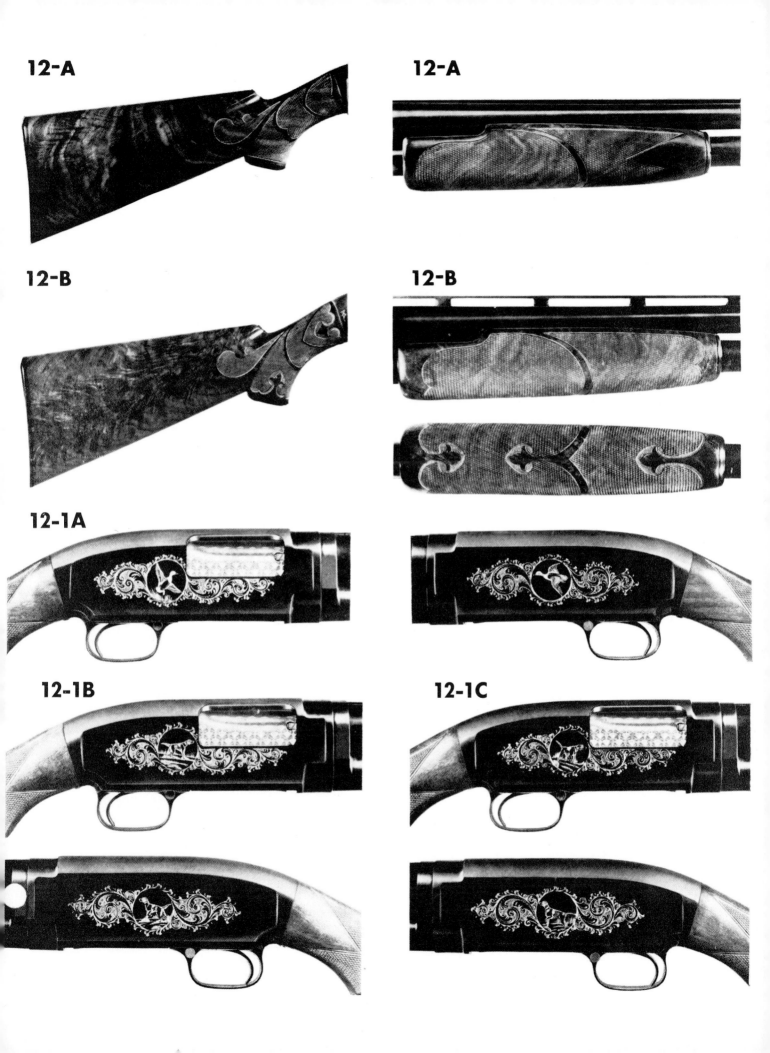

12-A

12-B

12-B

12-1A

12-1B

12-1C

Ranger shells, upper left, were introduced in 1925 in 12, 16 and 20 gauges, and in 1937 in 10 and 28 gauges. There was a post WW II run of Rangers in 24 gauge. All Ranger shells were red but some faded to light brown. The second Ranger shell, upper right, goes with the box label and was called Staynless. The new primers were the stainless element. The label is blue with red and white print. The box and shell below were introduced sometime before 1932. Note the battery cup primer. The label is red on white with black lettering.

Skeet loads were introduced in 1932 in 12, 16 and 20 gauges and in 1937 in 28 gauge. The box label is blue and red on yellow.

Super Skeet shells were introduced in 1940 in 12, 16 and 20 gauges. The box has a blue frame around a cream field and the print is red and blue.

Trap load Rangers were likely introduced about the same time as skeet loads. This blue and red on yellow box is pictured in the 1938 price list.

Super Trap shells were introduced in 12, 16 and 20 gauges in 1940. Both trap and skeet versions are still in the line in the form of Super Target shells without the Ranger designation. Note that just as there were 16 and 20 gauge trap guns, there were trap shells. This box is also yellow with blue and red labeling.

The 10 gauge box above with blue and red print on yellow was overprinted for use with black powder blanks. The box below was the first issued following WW II. These shells were star crimped. The label is yellow with red and blue print.

The last box logo for paper shells, except Super Target shells, is yellow with a red W and RANGER in a blue field. The specimen below is an export box, with primed empty. In the United States, Ranger empties were sold in 100's boxes, in 10, 12, 16, 20 and 28 gauges beginning in 1937. The 28 gauge was not listed after WW II, the others were discontinued in December 1950.

The Mark 5 Ranger was introduced in 1964. Smooth and rough plastic and smooth and corrugated brass were common. The label is yellow between red horizontal stripes, with blue shields for the RANGER and MARK 5. The last Ranger box below was very shiny. In 1973 Winchester and Western logos were merged and field load boxes and shell sides began to be labeled pertinent to the game for which they were intended; e.g. upland, dove, dove and quail, squirrel and rabbit, pheasant and duck. The label has a gold field between red, with blue shields for RANGER and MARK 5.

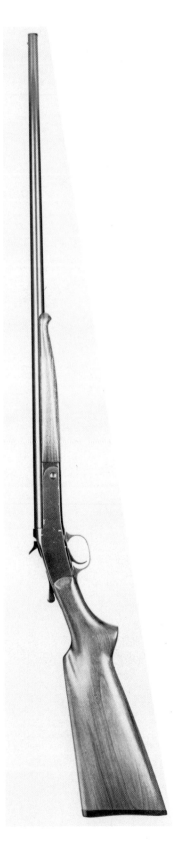

Chapter 8

MODELS 20, 36 AND 41

After World War I, Winchester had manufacturing capacity which could be devoted to sporting arms lines it had previously not pursued. In 1920, it introduced three small bore, single shot shotguns, which were destined to fail in the marketplace.

Model 20   1920–1924

The first Model 20's were delivered to the warehouse in March 1919. The Model 20 was Winchester's first break-down, top lever hammer gun and first .410 bore (2½ inch). The 1920 catalog contained the usual praiseful prose:

> The new Winchester .410 bore shotgun, Model 20 is designated for the shooter who wants a small-bore, single shotgun of high grade and superior workmanship. It has all the shooting qualities that the larger gauge guns possess within its effective range of 30 yards. It is especially adapted to practice shooting, small game hunting, and breaking the midget trap targets. The cost of ammunition is comparatively little.
>
> The Winchester .410 is an ideal gun for women and the younger members of the family to shoot because of its virtual absence of recoil and its light weight. These qualities have made it highly popular wherever it has been used.
>
> This gun has all the finish and balance of the Winchester standard size shotguns. It is made with the same care and accuracy. The barrel is of the highest grade gun steel, accurately bored, and bearing the Winchester Proof Mark of barrel quality.
>
> The stock of this gun is a handsome, well-finished, black walnut product, with pistol grip.
>
> The barrel of this gun is 26 inches long. The length of trigger pull is 13½ inches; drop at heel 2½ inches, and drop at comb 1⁹⁄₁₆ inches. The weight of the gun is about 6 pounds.

Winchester Junior Trapshooting Outfit

The same catalog introduced this little known and quite rare cased set as "a new shooting game for the entire family" and "the shooting novelty of the year for young and old."

> Besides the new and graceful .410 Winchester Shotgun, a little beauty and a fine arm, the outfit includes the Winchester Midget Hand Trap, with which the shooter can throw the little clay targets at which he shoots, or have them thrown for him by any companion of his outing; 150 Winchester .410 Loaded Shells; 100 Clay Targets; Steel Cleaning Rod; Gun Grease; Gun Oil and Rust Remover.

The Model 20 illustrated on p. 82 was a handsome gun. This is no. 19XXX, 26″. The Junior Trap outfit illustrated above was attractive and promoted with a large window display distributed to sporting goods and hardware dealers. Six boxes with the special logo shown left below containing 2″ no. 8 shells were included in the outfit. The target, below right, was factory misshapen out of round. The white splotch of paint made it appear to spin. This is one of the three logos used.

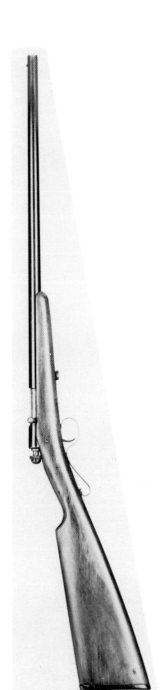

All packed in a rugged, handsome case, 30 × 8½ × 6 inches. The total weight of outfit complete, including everything necessary for the sport of trapshooting, is about 40 pounds.

This outfit was truly beautiful. In addition to the above items, it contained a brochure entitled "A Whole New Field of Sport," which described the outfit and how to set up a field for junior trapshooting, a 16 page booklet "How to Use and Care for the Winchester Junior Trapshooting Outfit," a miniature score pad, a 12 page booklet "Winchester Repeating Shotguns General Instructions," and instructions for using Winchester cleaning materials, the latter on oiled paper.

All guns were full choke. Fancy walnut and checking could be special ordered. The forearm had a lip at the front—not like a schnabel but more like an L. C. Smith single trap. The ejector was non-selective. At about 8000, it was made longer, the hinge pin was notched accordingly, and a flat was milled on the barrel just ahead of the lump.

At about 12000, the hammer checking was made longer and at about 19000 it was made coarser. At about 19000, the serial number was stamped only on the receiver. Earlier, it was also stamped on the trigger guard. Barrel markings also changed several times.

The January 2, 1930 Retail Price List listed "Stainless Steel Barrels" at $11.75 extra. Subsequent literature did not show this option.

Manufacture was discontinued in 1924, a few were assembled from 1925 to 1927, and the last guns were sold in 1931. According to Madis (1981, p. 213) 12,358 guns were made between 1927 and 1935, most of them for export. Approximately 23,616 were made. The Model 20 was first priced at $30.00 and was reduced to $16.50 in 1922. Because it was designed as a .410 it was well-proportioned unlike most competitive items, which were scaled down versions of 12 or 20 gauge guns. Yet, it was not competitive.

Model 36   1920–1927

The first single shot introduced in the March 1920 catalog was the Model 36. The first guns were delivered to the warehouse in March 1920. This gun was nearly identical to the Model 1902 rifle. This was Winchester's first bolt-action shotgun and its first arm with other than walnut stock. It was also the smallest Winchester shotgun. It was meant to be a garden or vermin gun. The catalog stated:

> This is a new Model Winchester shotgun designed for short range work with the 9 m/m ammunition, much used, in some localities, for this type of work. It is a bolt-action single shotgun, light in weight, and handy and economical for use. . .
>
> The Model 36 is a Take-Down type shotgun which can be taken apart simply by unscrewing the thumbscrew under the forearm which releases the action and barrel from the stock. The barrel is made of the finest gun steel, carefully bored, and bearing the Winchester Proof Mark of barrel perfection. The barrel is 18 inches long.
>
> This gun has a straight grip and the length of pull is 13⅛ inches; drop at comb, 1⅝ inches; drop at heel, 2⅞ inches . . . (Weight about 2¾ pounds).
>
> The Winchester shot cartridges, manufactured especially for this shotgun, are made in two sizes, the 9 m/m Rim Fire Long—sometimes known as double-charge, and the 9 m/m Rim Fire Short—or single-charge. Each is loaded with No. 9 shot. . . There is also made for this shotgun a 9 m/m Rim Fire ball cartridge. . .

The 9 mm shotshell was developed late in the nineteenth century. The chamber size was 9 mm and bore diameter was .309 inch. The shell body measured .314 inch and the rim diameter was .402 inch.

Special Notes

1. This gun was made up in standard style only. It was not serially marked and there were very few changes. The first firing pin head was cylindrical with coarse knurling. The later firing pin head was rounded at the rear and knurled at the front. Stocks were made of gum wood with a hard rubber butt plate with round logo and engraved screws. Standard barrels were 18 inches long. According to Madis (1981, p. 214) a few 17 inch barrels wre made in 1925.

2. Because 9 m/m rim fire ammunition was loaded with black powder, specimens with mirror bores are rare. The blue was prone to flaking and the gum wood stocks were inclined to warp. High quality specimens are rare—likely because many were stored in outbuildings where they were used to destroy pests.

3. Some early guns were sold in South America and in England. Occasionally, one with English proof marks is offered for sale.

Manufacture was discontinued in 1927 at 20,306. This number is definitely an approximation. Old factory records also recorded that 25,781 were made. The Model 36 was first listed at $13.00 and was reduced to $7.50, yet sales averaged less than 600 per year. This was a very specialized American shotgun and a very interesting addition to any Winchester collection. Ladies especially ask "What is that?" when they see one among full-sized guns.

The Model 36, opposite page, was a tiny shotgun. Note the later style firing pin head. Three special black powder loadings were made for the Model 36. They were introduced in 1916 and last listed in 1949. The 9mm long shotshells were red, green, yellow, or blue. All known 9mm short shotshells are blue. The ball cartridge was made in very small quantities. The box is red with black lettering.

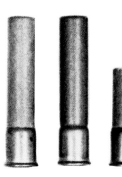

Model 41   1920–1934

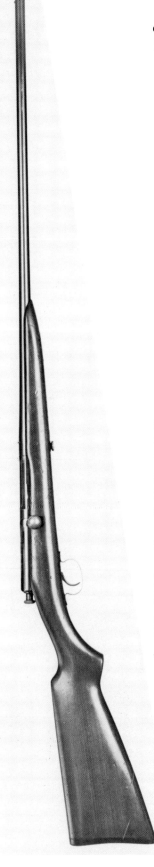

The second low-priced single shot shotgun to appear in the March 1920 catalogue was the Model 41. The first guns were delivered to the warehouse in 1920. The catalog told nearly all:

> For the lover of the small-bore shotgun the Winchester Repeating Arms Company has now developed a new shotgun of the bolt-action type, the first of this style of shotgun made in America that is of the highest grade in material, appearance, and shooting qualities. The action of this gun is of the "upturn and pull-back" type. . . .
>
> This gun is a two-piece Take-Down. It is taken apart very easily by unscrewing a small thumbscrew located under the forearm. It can be taken down and put together in a very few seconds. Taken down the barrel section is 31¾ inches long and the gun over all measures 44½ inches. . .
>
> This Bolt-Action .410 is as attractive a gun to shoot as it is to hold and operate. It has a 24-inch barrel, handsome pistol grip stock of black walnut, fitted with a rubber butt plate, and is pleasing in every line. The stock may be obtained in straight grip if so ordered, at no additional cost. Complete, the gun weighs slightly over 4½ pounds. It is strong, serviceable, hard hitting, and accurate up to the limit or range for a shotgun of this caliber.
>
> The length of trigger pull is 13½ inches; drop at comb 1¾ inches, and drop at heel 2¾ inches.

Special Notes

1. This gun was made up in standard style only. It was not serially marked and there were few changes. Sometime in 1933 chambering was changed to 3 inch. Catalog 89, 1934, lists only 3 inch chambering. Barrel markings changed from "PAT. APPLIED FOR" to "PAT. AUG. 17, 1920," and from "For 2½ inch shells" to "For 3 inch shells." All guns were full choke. A rear sight consisted of a thin blade with a shallow curved notch and was staked in a lateral groove just ahead of the loading port.

2. The January 2, 1930 Retail Price List listed "Stainless Steel Barrels" at $11.75 extra. Subsequent literature did not show this option.

Manufacture was discontinued in 1934 at approximately 22,146. According to Madis (1981, p. 216) parts cleanup from 1934 to 1941 brought total production to 23,335. The Model 41 was first listed at $14.00 and was reduced to $13.25. Approximately 1250 were sold each of the first four years. It was retained in the line longer than the Model 20 and Model 36, but sold no better.

The Model 41 was a sleek bolt action. This is a 3″ .410 bore with 24″ barrel.

Chapter 9

MODEL 21

Without question Winchester shotgun collectors covet the Model 21 above all other models. This is partly because of value, certainly because side-by-sides have special appeal, and likely because the 21 was made in more gauges and grades and with more styles of embellishment than any other Winchester shotgun. The Model 21 was inroduced with a lot of fanfare about several design features. The 1933 catalog summarized these:

> BARRELS—The barrel design of this new Winchester is one of its distinctive features and one that has much to do with the perfection of the barrels themselves. The barrels are dove-tailed together in a mechanical interlock which is far superior to brazing or any other union for there is no distortion or destruction of the temper and strength of the barrel by the terrific heat of brazing. This makes possible the retention of the tremendous strength due to the Winchester system of heat treating the barrels of this gun.
>
> Each barrel with its half lug is a single integral mass forged from Winchester-Proof steel, treated to have a tensile strength of 115,000 pounds per square inch. The barrel is bored and finished with the precision for which Winchester has always been justly famous. The two half-lugs, thus united by the dove-tailing process, form the locking lug of the barrel unit. Thus the locking bolt acts directly on the barrels themselves.
>
> Scientific methods, developed by Winchester experience and skill, maintain an unusual uniformity of barrel-wall thickness.

Model 21 Standard Grade with Double Triggers and Selective Ejection. Shown here in 20 Gauge.

The hollow matted top rib fits tightly over an upward projecting lug integral with the barrels at the rear, thus greatly strengthening the attachment of the top rib and permitting it to be one continuous piece from the muzzle to the breech.

BARREL STOP—In the forward part of the barrel lug is a floating barrel stop. This is the member that prevents the breech from opening too far. When the breech is opened this floating stop tilts and rotates slightly as it reaches the top shoulders of the frame so that the surfaces always meet evenly. Thus no excessive wear can be thrown on any narrow surface or edge nor can any bruising or battering, due to violent opening, take place. The barrel stop is practically unbreakable, thus avoiding the weak point in the structure of most break-down guns.

TOP LEVER—In the Winchester double gun there is a niche cut into the face of the standing breech to expose the upper end of the bolt catch when the barrels are removed and a simple pressure of the thumb nail will push the bolt catch down, allowing the top lever to swing back to a central position.

THE FRAME of this Winchester Double Gun is made, not of the usual case-hardened material, but of the Winchester PROOF STEEL treated to have a tensile strength of over ninety tons per square inch. We are confident that it will show no evidence of yielding at the breech after a lifetime of shooting with the heaviest modern loads.

The Frame

LOCKING BOLT SYSTEM—There is a widespread belief that when a double gun is fired the locking device is subjected to heavy strain. In a properly constructed gun this is not so. In proof of this we have fired heavy loads in the Winchester gun with the locking bolt removed and the barrels held down by the hand alone. With a frame as strong and well designed as is the Winchester frame, a single sturdy locking bolt is amply sufficient. No top lock being necessary on the Winchester double gun, Winchester was able to leave off all rearward projections on the breech of the barrels which interfere with the easy loading or removal of shells.

LOCKING BOLT—Is a single longitudinally sliding wedge-action bolt, housed immediately below the breech face of the frame and wedging into a cut in the rear face of the barrel lug and which forces down the breech of the barrels firmly on the frame table under the stress of the ample coiled bolt spring, but is so designed that it can neither stick nor allow the breech to open.

As ordinarily constructed, a bolt having an incline sufficiently steep to prevent sticking will jar loose under heavy loads, and if made with an incline so oblique as not to jar loose, will stick. To overcome this, Winchester uses a stop screw, located in the locking cut of the barrel and easily accessible when the gun is opened, which limits the travel of the locking bolt, thereby preventing sticking and which permits adjustment after long use to take up any trivial looseness due to wear.

The 1938 Winchester Model 21 catalog and other literature described demonstrations of shooting 21's with locking bolts removed and the barrels held down by hand or a cotton string. Shooting the gun with the locking bolt removed was not advertising malarky. I knew a Winchester representative who shot thousands of rounds at trap in the Chicago area with the bolt removed. Of course, this could be done with Model 21's primarily because the hinge pin was farther forward of

The first gun illustrated at right is a very early Model 21 Standard or Field Grade, 12 ga., 32″ barrels, with small forearm, double triggers and a stock which Frank Parker called a canoe paddle. The hinge pin on the Model 21 was farther forward than on other double shotguns, giving it great strength.

The second gun is a Standard or Field Grade, 12 ga., 32″. A very early gun with small forearm, single trigger, and the first style stock. Note that the checking pattern differs from the first gun. Because all Model 21 stocks were made by hand from machine-inletted blanks, details vary.

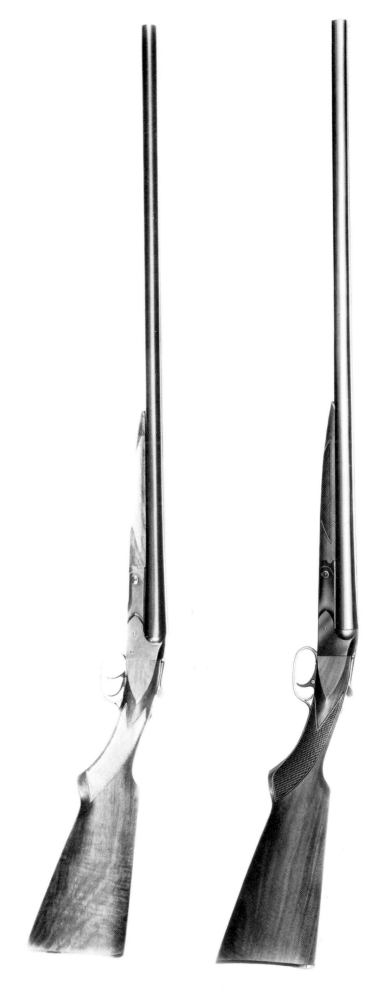

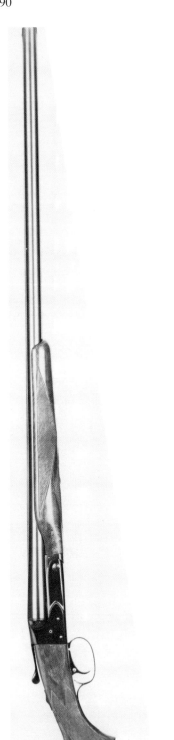

the breech than on other doubles. This also increased the effectiveness of the single bolt.

The 1933 catalog also described the selective ejectors and the single trigger.

> The Winchester double barrel shotgun, Model 21, is also furnished in Selective Ejection models, both in the double trigger and single trigger guns. In these numbers when the gun is opened either or both of the shells will be automatically ejected according to whether one or both shells have been fired.
>
> This Winchester Selective Ejection is simple and sturdy in design and therefore is not subject to mal-adjustment or failure by long, hard use. By its novel construction, when the breech is opened, the fired shell is thrown clear, while the unfired shell is pushed well out where it is readily grasped for removal if desired. If both shells are fired, both are ejected; if neither is fired, both are pushed part way out for easy removal and if one only is fired that shell is ejected only.
>
> The Winchester Single Trigger is made on an entirely new principle and is free from defects so often found in single triggers. It will neither "double" nor balk. To shoot right barrel first, simply push the gold shift button over so that it projects at the right side of the trigger. So long as the button is left in this position the first pull will fire the right barrel, whether the left is fired or not before re-loading. The lightest touch or glance will tell whether it is set for right barrel first or for left barrel first and it can be instantly shifted to either position even while raising the gun to fire.
>
> After firing the first barrel, fully releasing and again pulling the trigger will fire the second barrel. This full release of the trigger gives the shooter the same length of pull and feel for both barrels. In order to reverse the order of firing, that is to fire the left barrel first, simply push the gold button over to the left side.

The principal designer of the Model 21 was George Lewis. He was assisted by Thomas Crossley Johnson (who designed the Model 12) and William Roehmer. The Model 21 was conceived circa 1925 and not introduced until the depths of the great depression when Winchester was in dire financial straits. It was called Model 21 because it came after the Model 20, which was the first break-open gun made by Winchester. The first guns were completed in March 1930 and Winchester Repeating Arms Company declared bankruptcy about the same time. It was acquired by the Western Cartridge Company effective December 22, 1931. The Western leadership consisted of F. W. Olin and his two sons, John M. and Spencer T. Olin. According to Williamson (1952 p. 380) John M. Olin had been an admirer of Winchester firearms from boyhood. He toured the New Haven plant and learned a great deal about various models from Mr. Johnson. He saw (or hoped) for a great future for the Model 21 and ordered increased production in greater varieties. Nevertheless, little was spent to promote it prior to World War II and few were sold. Deluxe and custom grades were largely the result of Mr. Olin's concern to promote it as the finest side-by-side made. It is likely that he fostered the 28 gauge, 410 bore, and double rifles. In the 1970s, Mr. Olin was almost solely responsible for survival of the Model 21. In the late 1970s, the board of directors of Olin Corporation voted to discontinue the Custom Shop which was assembling high grade Model 12's and 21's. The decision was suspended on the request of Mr. Olin that Model 21's be made until his death.

Standard or Field Grade 1931–1959: 12, 16, 20 Gauge

The first Model 21's were delivered to the warehouse in March 1930. The January 2, 1931 "Rifles and Shotguns Retail Price List" introduced the Model 21

Duck Gun no. 29XXX, 12 ga., 30″, with solid rib, single trigger, no grip cap.

Double Barrel Hammerless Shotgun in standard grade with double trigger at $59.50. This price list was issued with the 1931 catalog, which made no mention of Model 21's. The next several catalogs stated—". . . the Model 21, will be available about April 1, 1931 in Selective Ejection Models, both in the double trigger and single trigger guns." Before then only twelve gauge double trigger guns were available. When introduced, standard grade guns had pistol grips, small forearms, and rubber butt plates. They were furnished with automatic safeties but could be ordered with non-automatic safeties at no charge. Post-war catalogs shifted the term standard grade to field grade.

Tournament Grade 1932–1936: 12, 16, 20 Gauge

This grade began as a special order gun. Stocks were made to customer specifications within certain limits and could include beavertail forearm, Monte Carlo, cheek piece, and offset. After 1933, guns with standard barrel length and choke combinations were supplied from stock with standard dimensions, but guns could still be ordered to specification. Twelve gauge guns could be had in 26, 28, 30, or 32 inch barrel lengths and 16 and 20 gauge guns could be had in 26, 28, or 30 inch. The 12 gauge 32 inch gun could be furnished with a ventilated rib. In 1933, the 26 inch skeet gun with straight or pistol grip, checked butt, and beavertail forearm was introduced. Non-automatic safeties were standard on skeet guns. They were furnished without safeties at no extra charge.

Trap Grade 1932–1938: 12, 16, 20 Gauge
1942–1959: 12 Gauge

Early Trap grade guns could be had with single or double triggers, extractors or selective ejectors, straight or pistol grips, customer specified stock dimensions, and choice of several recoil pads. The major difference from tournament grade guns was higher quality walnut. Trap grade skeet guns (same features as Tournament grade skeet guns but finer wood) were available after 1933. Some 20 gauge Trap grade guns had extra 28 gauge barrels. All of these examined were bored WS-1 and WS-2. Ventilated 30 inch barrels were added in 1933. The 1938 catalog stated that 16 and 20 gauge Trap grade guns could be special ordered and the Trap gun page had "DISCONTINUED" over-printed in red. The 1940 catalog listed only 12 gauge trap guns with non-automatic safeties as standard-automatic or no safety on special order. Post-war catalogs listed 12 gauge Trap guns. These were not special order guns.

Custom Built Grade 1933–1940: 12, 16, 20 Gauge

All of the options available on other grades were available on custom built guns. Stock dimensions, engraving, gold and silver inlay, and carving were done to customer choice from standard patterns or (likely within some limits) from customer designs. The Winchester Model 21 catalogs stressed individual satisfaction with engraving, carving, dimensions, and even color of wood. One of the custom built guns pictured in these catalogs had a scalloped junction of frame and butt stock. This was likely one of a kind, but even if several were made, they would be extremely rare and valuable. Until 1938 only 12 gauge guns could be had with ventilated ribs.

A factory loaded 16 gauge 3″ shell. Some 16 gauge Model 21's were bored for 3″ shells.

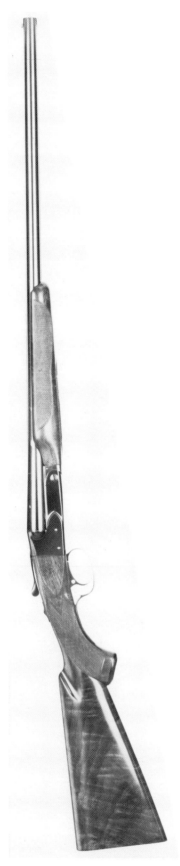

Skeet Gun 1933–1959: 12, 16, 20, 28 Gauge

The 1933 catalog and subsequent literature listed skeet guns. Usually, separate sections showed straight and pistol grip guns. Thus, for a time guns for skeet could be had in tournament, trap, custom or skeet. Skeet guns were nearly like field grade guns. The wood was usually not as fancy as on trap guns, although there are exceptions. Some had hard rubber pistol grip caps. Only a few were 28 gauge.

Duck Gun 1940–1954: 12 Gauge 3″

Three inch chambers could be had in 12, 16, and 20 gauge guns on special order after 1932. Winchester Leader three inch 16 gauge shells exist from this period and at least one gun is known. The duck gun was furnished with 30 or 32 inch full choke raised matted rib barrels, pistol grip stock, Winchester rubber recoil pad, automatic safety, and standard stock dimensions. Special dimension straight or pistol grip stocks were furnished without extra charge. Ventilated ribs were furnished at extra charge.

Deluxe Grade 1942–1951: 12, 16, 20 Gauge

The October 1946 Retail Price List stated that "Model 21 Deluxe Shotguns will be furnished in any of the standard Model 21 shotgun styles and in accordance with the standard specifications and regularly allowed options as shown on pages covering each style: Standard or Field Guns, Skeet Guns, Trap Guns, Duck Guns. All Model 21 Shotguns will be made with 1—Single triggers and selective ejectors. 2—Hand made stocks to customer's dimensions. 3—Stocks and forearms of full fancy American walnut with fancy deluxe checking. 4—Smoothed working parts." Extras for deluxe grade guns were: beavertail forearm on field gun, ventilated rib, special rounded frame, six styles of engraving, two styles of carving, name plates, various recoil pads, and gold plated trigger.

The December 15, 1950 Wholesale-Retail Price List and General Catalog devoted two pages to the Model 21 Deluxe and also called it the *Model 21 Custom Deluxe*.

Custom Built 1952–1959

The January 2, 1952 catalog listed Model 21's with "Custom Built by Winchester" engraved on the top rib. This feature was continued on custom, pigeon, and Grand American grade guns after 1959. Custom built guns were available with all the options available on what catalogs called deluxe and deluxe custom guns. Page 66 of the 1955 catalog (which was especially fancy and played on a century of development beginning wih the Volcanic Rifle in 1855) was devoted to the Custom Built .410 bore. All .410's were custom built (but not all custom built guns were fancy). Page 66 claimed that the .410 "frame is smaller and lighter, and is available only with 26″ Ventilated Rib Barrels—any chokes." The 1959 catalog was the last to list the .410 bore.

Skeet Gun no. 16XXX, 16 ga., 26″. Solid rib, checked butt, and hard rubber grip cap. This is exceptionally fine grain wood for this grade.

The .410 bore and 28 gauge guns were made on 20 gauge frames. Most .410's were made with custom or round frames. A few .410 barrels were fitted to "tear drop" frames. Both .410 bore and 28 gauge guns were made in less than custom grade. Sets were made up with sets of barrels in two gauges, and rarely .410, 28, and 20. Four guns of special interest are: (1) Mr. Olin's gun number 25087 made in December 1950 with 26 and 28 inch .410 bore skeet-and-skeet barrels. In April 1955 it was fitted with 26 inch full and modified .410 bore barrels and in August 1955 it was fitted with full and modified 28 gauge, and skeet and skeet 28 gauge barrels—five sets in all, tightest chokes in the right barrels for quickest recovery for the second shot; (2) Number 32560, which is the only known .410/28 cased Grand American; (3) Number 32625, which is a .410/28 Grand American with raised gold; (4) Number 32566, which is a .410/28/20.

Magnum Gun 1954–1959, 3 inch: 12 and 20 Gauge

The 1953 Wholesale-Retail Price List called the 12 gauge magnum "Model 21 Magnum" but did not show the 20 gauge magnum. The January 2, 1954 catalog listed the Model 21 Magnum Gun with raised matted or ventilated rib barrels in 12 gauge with 32 or 30 inch barrels and 20 gauge with 30 inch barrels and three inch chambers. Many 20 gauge barrels are marked "For 2¾ inch and 3 inch Shells." These were completed guns which were rechambered and marked at the factory as orders came in for magnum 20's.

Custom, Pigeon, Grand American Grades 1960-1982: 12, 16, 20 Gauge

Production of Model 21's in the regular grades ceased in 1960. From then on Custom, Pigeon, and Grand American grade guns were made in the new location in the factory called the Custom Shop. Only frame polishing was done across the street in the old location. Literature of 1960 inroduced these three grades. They were available, in 12, 16, and 20 gauge with standard barrel lengths and any choke combination. Custom grade guns were first listed with matted ribs (but many were made with ventilated ribs) 2¾ inch chambers, rounded frames, AA full fancy wood made to custom specifications, black insert in forearm tip, fancy checking, steel grip cap, composition butt plate, recoil pad, or checked butt, automatic or non-automatic safety, choice of various bead sights, engine turning on certain surfaces, custom style engraving, gold plated trigger, and gold oval name plate (optional) with three initials. The top rib was marked "Custom Built by Winchester for (customer's name)."

Pigeon guns were listed with all of the above features plus matted or ventilated ribs and 2¾ or 3 inch chambers (2¾ only on 16 gauge), full leather covering on recoil pad (optional), style "A" carving, #6 engraving, gold engraved pistol grip cap, and gold oval name plate or three initials gold inlaid on trigger guard. Gold on Model 21's was 24 carat.

Grand American grade guns were listed with all of the above features plus style "B" carving, #6 engraving with figures gold inlaid, set of interchangeable barrels with forearm, and Herkert and Meisel leather trunk case with canvas cover. Both case and cover were embossed with three initials in gold or black. Pistol grip caps had "Grand American" inlaid in gold. Some straight grip guns were issued with such a grip cap loose in the case. A few had "Grand American" inlaid in gold in the trigger guard tang.

Custom and Grand American Grades
12, 16, 20, 28 Gauge and .410 Bore 1982–

In late 1982, U.S. Repeating Arms Company announced major changes in Model 21 options. 12, 16, and 20 gauge guns were offered in Custom Grade at $9500.00 and Grand American Grade at $19,500.00. Pigeon Grade was discontinued. The Grand American Grade was also offered in 28 gauge or .410 bore at $30,000.00 and at $35,000.00 if fitted with one set of 28 gauge and one set of .410 bore barrels. *And,* eight Grand American Grade small bore sets (one set of barrels each in 20 and 28 gauge and .410 bore) were offered at $50,600.00. Literature indicated that on Model 21's valued at $19,000.00 or more a representative would, on request, come to the customer for personal fitting. Only one of the eight had been contracted for by mid-1983. Some potential customers were offered Model 21's with little embellishment at $7500. There was no factory engraver. By late summer of 1983, indebtedness and payroll obligations caused moves such as furloughs to ease a dire financial situation.

The note below concerns barrels available before the 1982 offering.

Special Notes

1. Barrels and ribs: At on time or another all barrels were made with both raised matted ribs (RMR) and ventilated ribs (VR). They were introduced as follows:

12 gauge: RMR 32″, 30″, 28″, 1931
VR 32″ 1932, 30″ 1933, 26″ 1938, 28″ 1947

16 gauge: RMR 30″, 28″, 26″ 1931
VR 26″ 1938, 28″ 1947
Some early ones had three inch chambers.

20 gauge: Same as 16 gauge. A few were made with 32 inch barrels. Some early ones and magnum guns had three inch chambers.

28 gauge: Added in 1936; date of discontinuance not known. RMR and VR and 26 and a few 28 inch were made. The 28 gauge barrels are heavy and make guns handle like double rifles. They were fitted to 20 gauge frames. Many had skeet chokes. The number made is unknown but likely about 200.

.410 bore: Listed in 1955, date of discontinuance not known. RMR and VR and 26 and 28 inch as well as 2½ and 3 inch chambers were made. Based on how his gun handled, Mr. Olin decided that 28 inch barrels were too muzzle heavy. Subsequently, none were made. The .410 bore barrels were light and curved from the width of the 20 gauge breech to a narrow muzzle. Frames and barrels were made lighter via vertical mill cuts in the water table and corresponding places under the breech. The number made is unknown but likely about 100.

2. Chokes: After 1931 all standard chokes were available. Skeet 1 and 2 were introduced in 1933, and special and custom order guns could be had with any choke combinations. Some weird combinations were made. A few live bird guns were bored full and improved modified so that right handers could shoot the near barrel first, to improve cheeking for the second shot. Some three inch guns did not have a full choke barrel because large shot does not require so much constriction.

3. Many guns had the grade stamped near the screw on the trigger plate. At least the following will be found: TOURNAMENT, TRAP, SKEET, TRAP/SKEET, DELUXE, DELUXE TRAP, DUCK. Post 1952 custom and higher

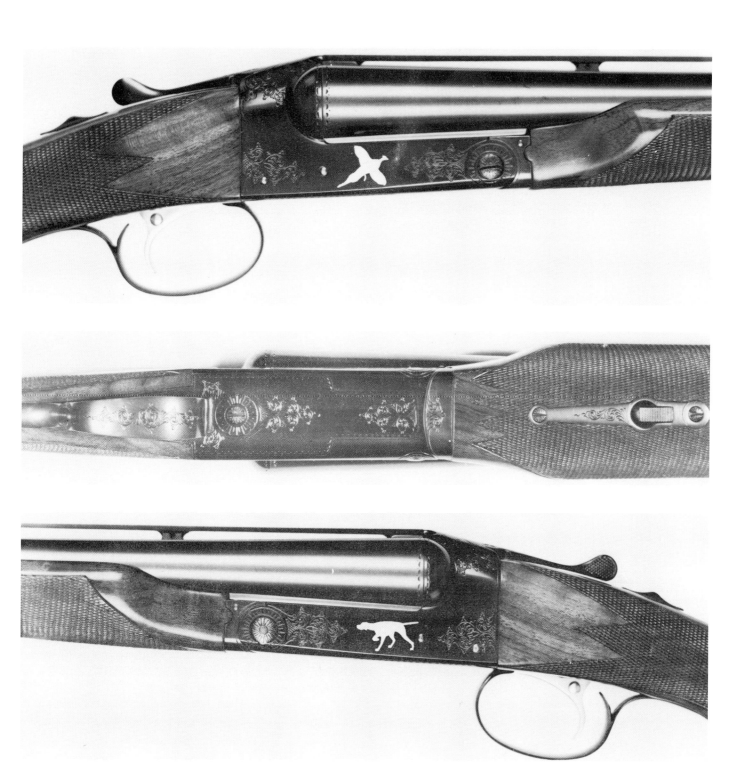

Custom Built no. 22XXX, 12 ga., 26″. This gun was shipped on January 14, 1969. It has standard Custom Grade engraving with gold figures extra. This recoil pad made by Pachmayer with a Winchester logo was used for a very brief period. Custom grade guns have fine wood to metal fit and finish. Engraving is tasteful but not profuse.

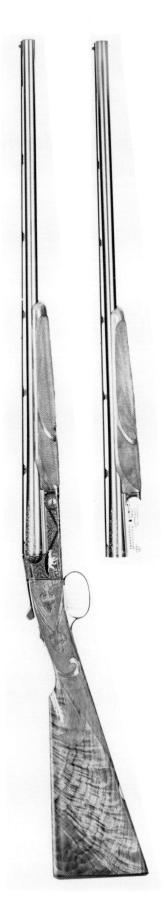

grades have "Custom Built by Winchester" on the top rib. These stampings were by no means used at all times. For example, three inch guns with no markings are common, with wide ranging serial numbers. Marking practices probably varied with the personnel making guns up at the time.

4. Wood: Early wood was very traditional in shape. Mr. John Olin told Grant Tom that in 1934 he and Frank Parker shared a duck blind, each with his pet double. Inevitably Mr. Parker commented that the 21 was a good looking gun, except for the stock which looked like a canoe paddle. Consequently, Model 21 stocks were reshaped. The comb was made higher and the pistol grip was made with a tighter curve, yet thin in cross section. The exterior of all Model 21 butt stocks was hand shaped.

Small forearms were available even afer World War II. Checking on beavertail forearms changed only once. The early pattern had curved borders and was called the kidney pattern. Later ones had diamond shaped borders. Hard rubber grip caps were used on some high grade guns until about 1955, then cast steel grip caps were used. For a time stamped steel caps were used. Later the cast steel cap was again used. Trap guns, for example, are found with and without grip caps in the same serial ranges. Straight or pistol grip stocks were always available without extra charge.

Several very odd-shaped stocks and forearms were made to customer specifications. One trap gun was made up with wood shaped like that on L. C. Smith singles. In 1969, Nick Kusmit, a factory engraver, showed me many pictures of guns with special wood or engraving. Pictures helped customers to consider the full range of options.

In 1941 two lengths of beavertail forearms were authorized for 12 gauge guns; 26 and 28 inch barrels were fitted with shorter forearms than were 30 and 32 inch barrels. No double ever had a more comfortable or more attractive forearm. The 20 and 28 skeet and .410 bore forearms were less full at the front.

5. Mechanical features: The only mechanical options were selective ejectors or extractors, single or double triggers, and automatic safety, non-automatic safety, or no safety. Extractors were discontinued in 1941 and double triggers were discontinued in 1944. On January 1, 1950, Winchester announced that Model 21's would be furnished only with selective ejectors and single triggers. Double triggers, however, were sometimes fitted to special guns. For example, in 1969 a 16 gauge pigeon grade was fitted with double triggers. Mr. Olin ordered this gun for presentation to an acquaintance.

The Model 21 was a stout gun. A few devoted trap and skeet shooters shot them many tens of thousands of times with little wear or breakage. It was rumored that 21's doubled. They absolutely did not, unless a blacksmith lightened the pulls by bending sear springs instead of changing sear angles with a hone. Pulls could be adjusted to less than three pounds by qualified smiths. Model 21's could readily be fitted with release triggers which could be easily removed and put back. Early beavertail forearms came loose from the iron and some cracked. This problem was eliminated with a long screw and abutment visible only from inside the forearm. The one weakness of early guns was fastening of the forearm lug. This was corrected by a key cut in the barrels. The lug was soldered in the key and could not move forward. When a 21 got loose it was a simple matter for a qualified smith to install a new bolt and/or hinge pin bushing, which were available in several sizes.

6. Kick: It is rumored that 21's kick more than similar guns. Kick is a simple matter of physics. Given proper stock dimensions (which were certainly available on 21's) recoil is a matter of force of explosion versus weight. Model 21's can be fitted and weighted to make recoil as imperceptible as from any gun. Quite a few 21 shooters made trap doubles look easy. Doubles are not easy if a gun hurts the shoulder.

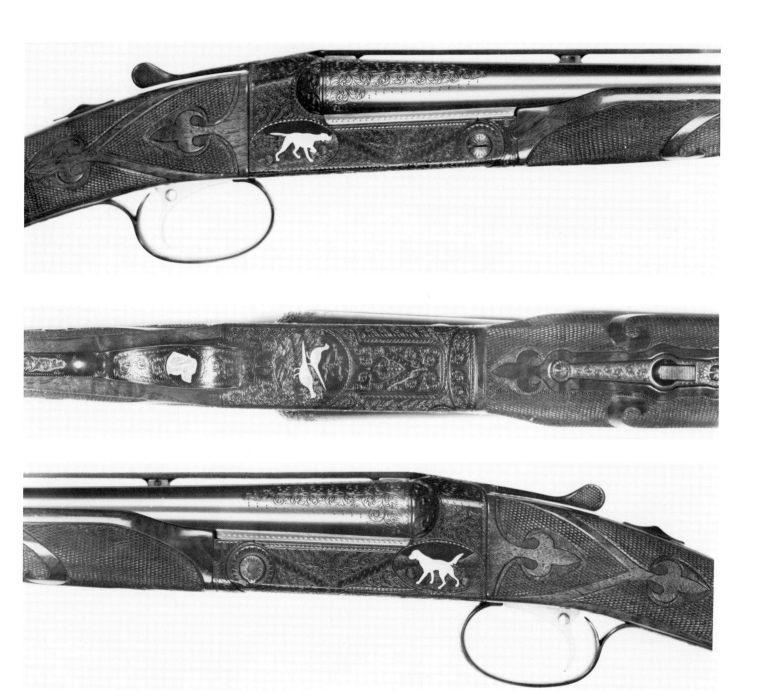

Custom Built no. 32XXX, 28 ga., 26″ and 20 ga., 26″. This gun was first shipped in November 1967. In 1973 it was factory upgraded like its .410 bore mate. Since then it has remained unfired. In 1979 it was fitted with the 20 gauge barrels. Number 6 engraving required approximately one week's work. This gun has all the features of a Grand American.

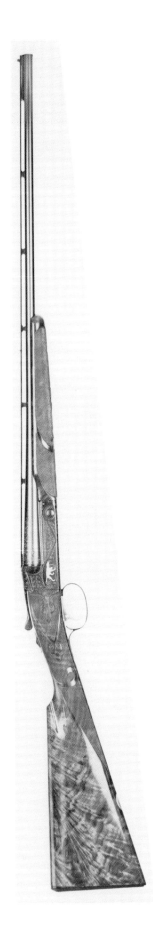

7. Double rifles: Two 21's were fitted with .405 W.C.F. rifled barrels. One is in the Winchester Museum, and it is rumored that a Chicago contractor once owned the other one. According to McIntosh (1981, p. 138) Winchester planned to make double rifle Model 21's from the start but was deterred by the depression. Research director Edwin Pugsley kept the idea alive. The two known double rifles were made on 20 gauge frames with double triggers and small forearms. Model 1895 caliber .405 W.C.F. barrels were lathe-turned to make liners for 26 inch 20 gauge barrels.

8. The Model 21's strength was demonstrated with two thousand 12 gauge proof loads. Mr. Olin gathered double guns from around the world and randomly selected a 21 from the warehouse. McIntosh (1982, pp. 21–22) reported that a Purdey lasted through 60 shots and that a BSA gave up at 150. After 2000 rounds at pressures one and one half times those of regular maximum loads, the 21 was disassembled, gauged, and found to be unscathed in any way. Page 10 of the 1938 Winchester Model 21 catalog showed the 2000 empty proof shells. These loads developed 7½ long tons pressure per square inch. Nearly 50 years after the test, Mr. Olin wrote Grant Tom saying "There was no near competitor in strength nor endurance to the Model 21." A far less modest statement was made by a trap shooter who shot more than 100,000 rounds in a 21, "No other break open gun would go so far without some gunsmithing." This is patently true of side-by-sides and nearly all over and unders.

9. Homer Clark Sr. of Alton, Illinois and a Model 21 made history. For some time prior to 1933 he shot trap doubles with a Marlin slide action. When he joined Western Cartridge Corporation, he was sent a Model 21. While practicing doubles with it, he remarked that one should be able to break a hundred straight with it because one could be sure the second shot was there when he wanted it. Then he went to the 1933 Kentucky State Shoot at Hill Top Gun Club in Paris. He broke the first 100 straight in a 50-pair race. (Mark Arie, from Thomasboro, Illinois, had broken 100 straight in a 100-pair event seven years before.)

Homer Clark, Jr. related the above at the Grand American in 1981. He used a Model 21 for a short time and had nothing but praise for it. Of course, he had to use Ithaca guns when he was employed by that firm. He won the world live bird championship twice with his Ithaca.

10. Only a few engravers worked on Model 21's. George Ulrich engraved the early guns. He designed the Grand American engraving, which earlier was 21-6 engraving. He died in 1949. In 1938, John Kusmit began training under Ulrich. He trained his younger brother Nick Kusmit (whose first job was sweeper) beginning in 1953. At the peak of his career, John Kusmit was the best. Nick Kusmit was next. Three other engravers were Jasper Salerno, Hank Bonham and Joe Crawley. In 1982 the only engraver was Pauline Muerrle.

11. Hints for collecting: Be careful about engraving. Probably no other American gun has been worked on by more custom engravers. Match engraving with pictures of factory engraving, but appreciate that many engravers copy factory designs. Also appreciate that many guns and especially early custom built guns were engraved to customer specifications. Winchester offered to send pictures so that customers could specify exactly what they wanted. Generally, factory engraving will be found together with better than field or skeet wood. Be leery of plain wood and #5 or #6 engraving. Do not be leery of what looks like factory gold on less than Grand American grade guns. Quite a few custom grade guns have factory gold figures. Factory gold or silver figures were raised until the mid 1950's after which they were flat. If in doubt, call or write the Winchester Museum to learn how the gun came from the factory. Factory engraving is desirable even if it was added, and many guns *were* returned to the factory for upgrading. This is especially true of 28 gauge and .410 bore guns. Such guns

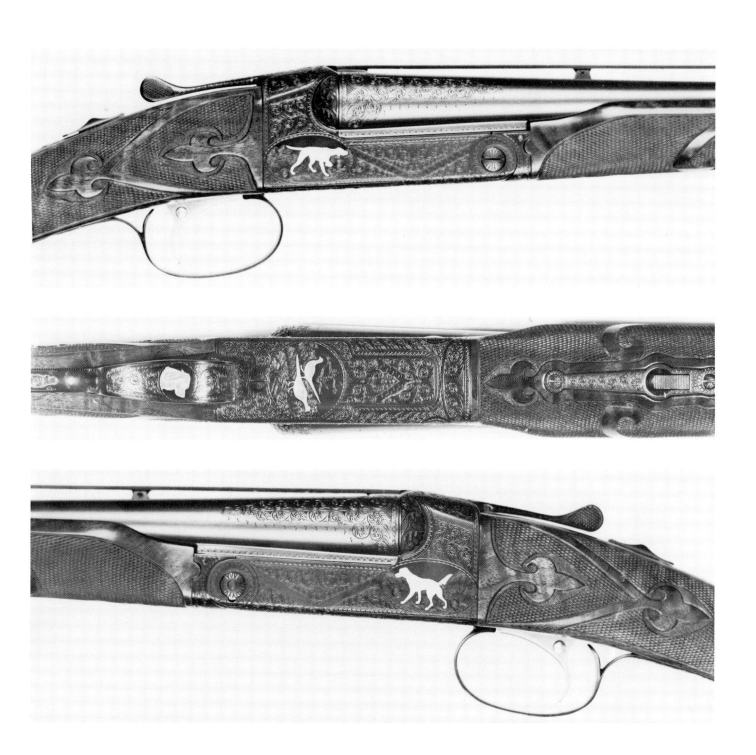

Custom Built no. 31XXX, .410 bore, 26″. This gun was first shipped in January 1959. In 1973 it was factory upgraded with 21-6 engraving and gold inlay, and 21-B carving. Since then it has remained unfired. This gun is an exact mate to the 28/20 gauge.

should be authenticated with factory letters and/or invoices for the upgrading work.

Also be careful about wood. Factory grips are thin. Study pictures of factory wood and especially checking patterns. If you are not satisfied that wood is original, look for the serial number inside the forearm wood. And, if you can get permission to have an excellent smith disassemble the piece, look in the groove for the guard. While you are inside, look for the metal sleeve in the hole for the large tang screw. Few custom stocks have this sleeve. Also, check the locks and the single trigger for rust. You do not want a gun which has been soaked or used near salt water without proper care.

Check the barrels. Length should be exactly 26, 28, 30, or 32 inches. Also check the chokes. Many clay target and live bird shooters had chokes opened. Clean the barrels. Then, look at a bright light from the breech end. You should be able to see the conical surfaces of the chokes. Even a little honing obliterates the junction of the parallel bore and the conical choke surfaces. No amount of shooting does.

Model 21 serial numbers go over 36,000. But, many numbered 16 gauge frames remain in the factory. A conservative estimate of the number of guns completed is 27,000. Thus, almost any original gun which has not been badly abused is a collector's item. Pay special attention to the small gauges.

In 1978, Pete Harvey paid $31,500 at auction for number 32667, a .410 skeet gun in Grand American grade (one set of barrels). This gun was made up by Winchester and auctioned to benefit the Winchester Museum. According to McIntosh (1981, p. 143) this gun then changed hands for $42,000, $48,000, and $60,000. It was subsequently sold for $94,000. In February 1982 it was offered for $125,000. It is likely that 28 gauge guns which can be had for less than $5,000 or .410 bore guns which can be had for less than $25,000 will appreciate nicely. There are also some good buys in 16 gauge guns. They are generally cheaper than similarly embellished 12 or 20 gauge guns and are likely to be more dear when all but a few 21's are in established collections.

Trap Grade no. 28XXX, 12 ga., 30″ with Winchester Ventilated Rib, pad, and first steel grip cap.

Engravings and Carvings for
Winchester Model 21 Custom Grade Double Barrel Shotguns

21 *Custom Engraving*

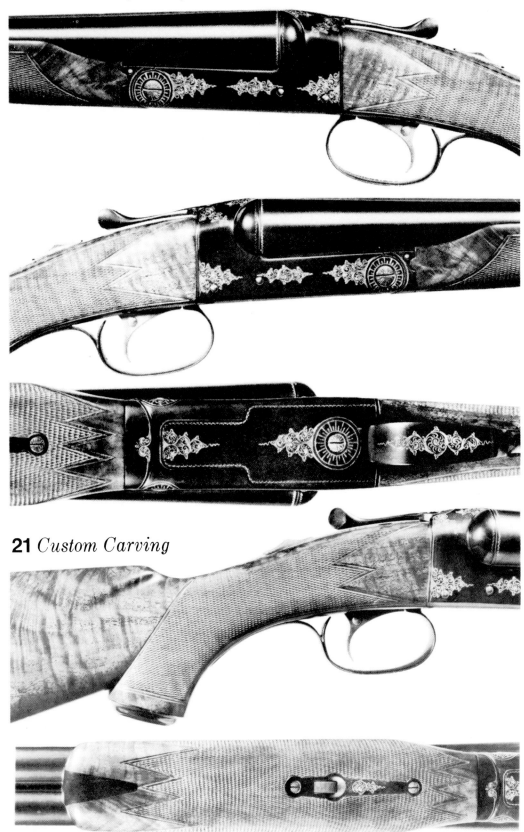

21 *Custom Carving*

Engravings for Winchester Model 21 Double Barrel Shotguns

21-3 *Engraving*

21-4 *Engraving*

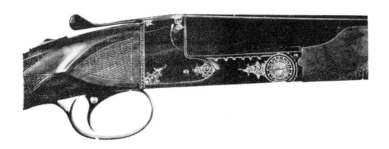

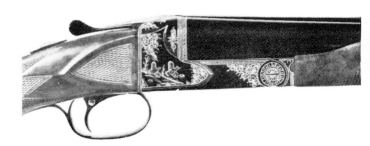

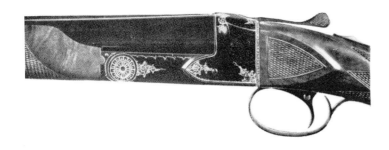

21-5 *Engraving*

21-6 *Engraving*

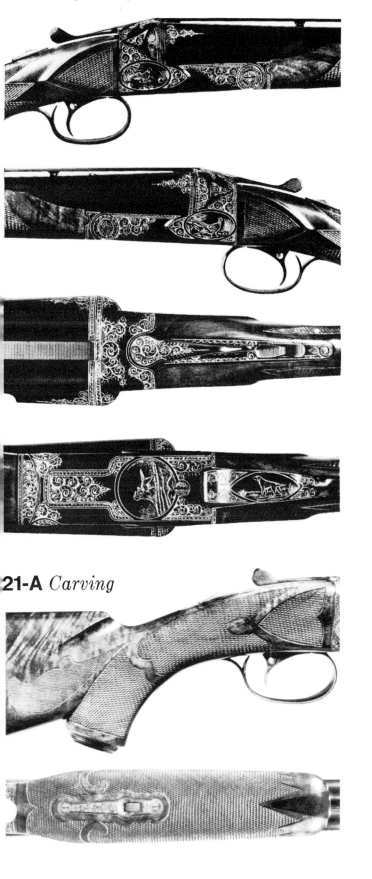

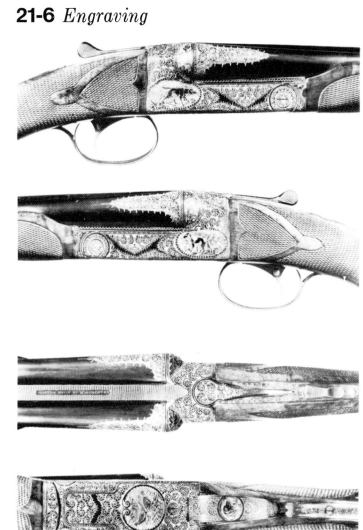

21-A *Carving*

21-B *Carving*

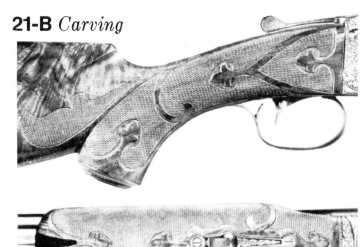

104

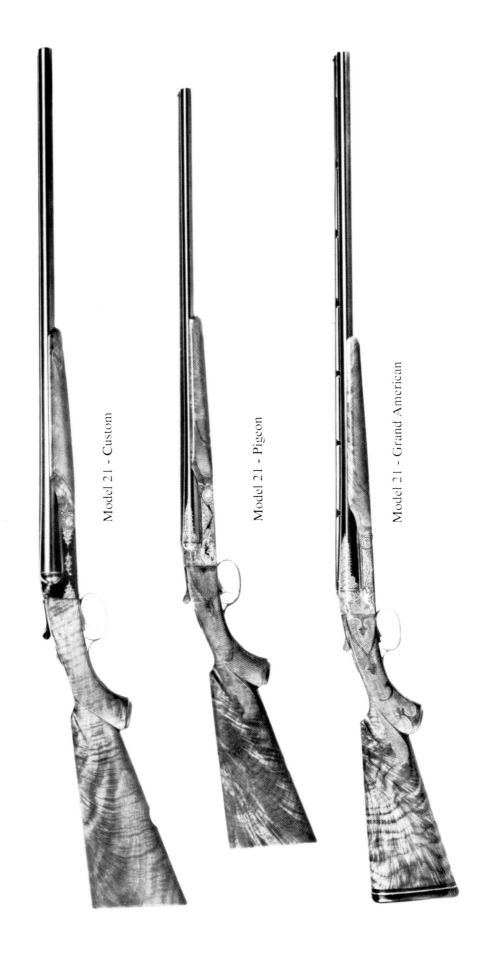

Model 21 - Custom

Model 21 - Pigeon

Model 21 - Grand American

SPECIFICATIONS NEEDED FOR YOUR
WINCHESTER® MODEL 21

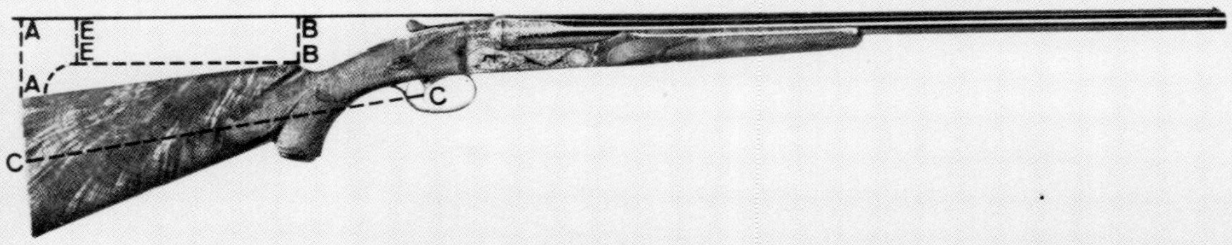

Ordered for: _____

Address: _____

By: _____ Date: _____

Grade: _____

Gauge: _____ Barrel Length: _____

Choke (Right): _____

Choke (Left): _____

RIB: ☐ Matted   ☐ Ventilated*

SAFETY: ☐ Automatic   ☐ Non-Automatic

CHAMBER: ☐ 2¾"   ☐ 3"*

SIGHTS:

	Front	Middle
Metal	☐	☐
Ivory Bead	☐	☐
Red Bead	☐	☐

FOREARM: ☐ Field   ☐ Trap   ☐ Skeet

BUTT: ☐ Butt plate   ☐ Checkered Wood   ☐ Recoil Pad

LEATHER COVERED PAD*: ☐ Faced   ☐ Slightly Rounded Edges   ☐ Fully Rounded Edges

Other Specifications or Information: _____

*On Pigeon & Grand American grades without extra cost

KIND OF STOCK: ☐ Pistol Grip   ☐ Straight Grip

Stock:

Length of Pull (C to C) _____   Drop at Comb (B to B) _____

Drop at Heel (A to A) _____   Drop at Monte Carlo (E to E) _____

Pitch _____

Information on cheekpiece, offset or other special dimensioning: _____

SHAPE OF COMB: ☐ Thin   ☐ Medium

OPTIONAL: Check One

☐ Initials on Trigger Guard

☐ Gold Oval Name Plate in underside of stock with initials

Initials Desired _____

Is name desired on rib panel? _____   If so, specify exactly as it is to

appear: _____

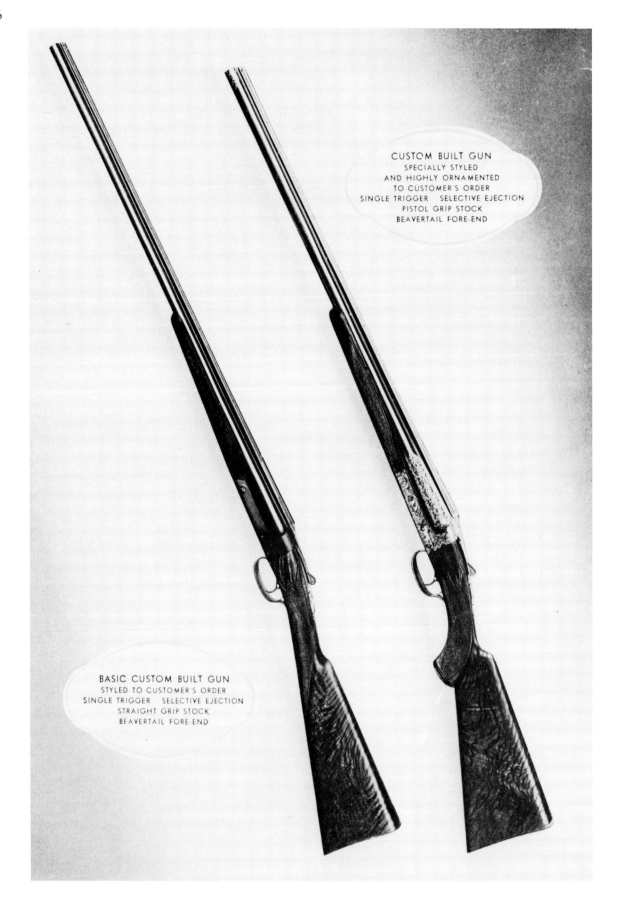

CUSTOM BUILT GUN
SPECIALLY STYLED
AND HIGHLY ORNAMENTED
TO CUSTOMER'S ORDER
SINGLE TRIGGER   SELECTIVE EJECTION
PISTOL GRIP STOCK
BEAVERTAIL FORE-END

BASIC CUSTOM BUILT GUN
STYLED TO CUSTOMER'S ORDER
SINGLE TRIGGER   SELECTIVE EJECTION
STRAIGHT GRIP STOCK
BEAVERTAIL FORE-END

The 1938 Winchester Model 21 catalog illustrated an ornate custom built specimen (above right) with scalloped-edge frame meeting the wood. This undoubtedly is one of a kind.

These photos illustrate the proof test discussed on p. 98. Note the hydraulic cylinder which absorbs recoil, and the box of proof shells. The lower illustration shows the gun after the test with 2000 empty proof shells. This was more punishment than any double gun has been subjected to before or since. The Model 21 cannot be over-rated for stout. The Leader proof shell is distinguishable by its tinned base.

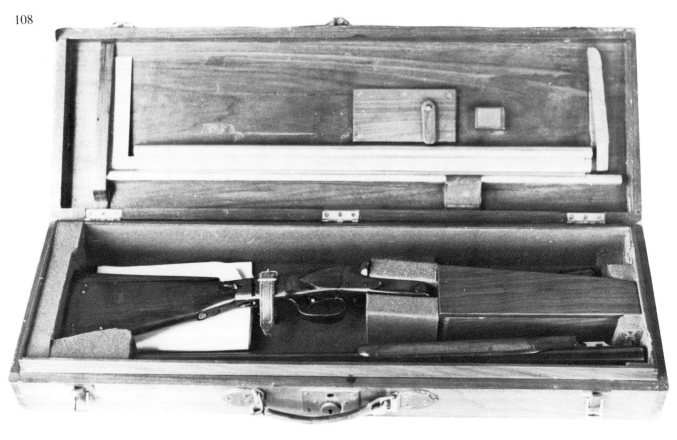

There are at least two try guns. Number two was cased in a rather crude walnut box with a brass name plate stamped "Try Gun No. 2, Property of Winchester Repeating Arms Co., New Haven, Conn." The box contained the gun, a screw driver for adjusting the stock, instructions for fitting/trying, a long two-piece stainless steel square for measuring drop and pitch, a steel tape, and aluminum brackets for displaying the gun above the box, probably at sports shows and the like. There was an empty place for a second set of barrels. This 20 gauge with 26 inch barrels was number 8572. A high level Olin employee stated emphatically that this was the only 20 gauge try gun. Try guns were shipped to representatives for fitting people who ordered high grade Model 21's. Then they were returned to New Haven. Thus, there may be only two—one 12 and one 20. Most shooters would have trouble shooting a try gun because the butt is very heavy.

Super Speed shells were introducd in 10, 12, 16, 20, 28, .410 2½ and .410 3″ in 1937. The box background above is yellow and red with blue and red print. The first post-war Super Speed box below contained the star crimped paper shell. It is yellow and red with blue and red print.

The last box logo for paper shells, above. The background is yellow, the print red and blue. The Mark 5 Super Speed was introduced in 1964. Smooth and rough plastic and smooth and corrugated brass were common. In 1973 Winchester and Western logos were merged. The high-powered shells became Winchester-Western Super X. The box label background is yellow, the print red and blue.

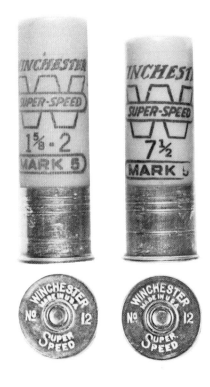

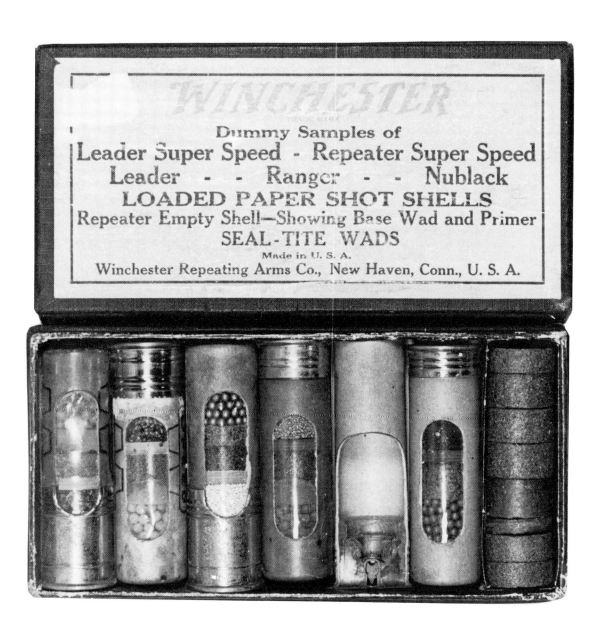

Box window shells produced ca 1933 showing the types available at the time. The column at right is wad samples.

112

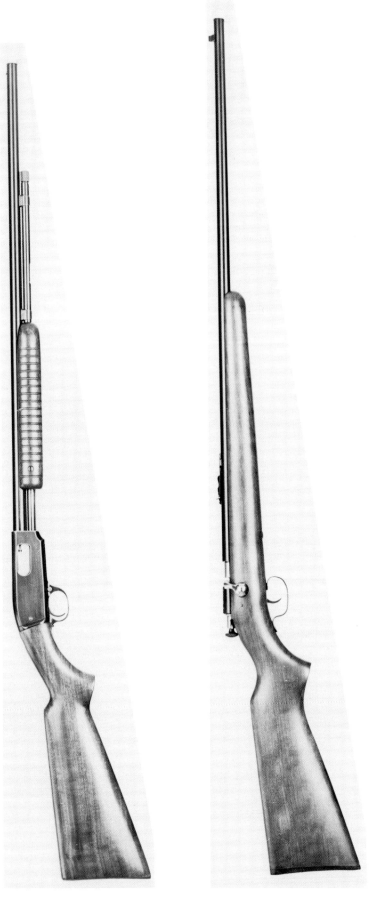

Smoothbore Model 61 no. 50XXX at left, with standard features, smooth receiver top.

Smoothbore Model 67 with standard features, including rifle sights.

Chapter 10
MODELS 61 AND 67

Two .22 caliber rim fire rifles were chambered for shot cartridges. These little known shotguns were used for pest control and target shooting.

Model 61, 1940–1960

The Model 61 was first listed in 1932. According to Madis (1981, p. 237) it was first bored for .22 shot when serials reched the mid 20,000's around 1937. The 1940 (undated form no. 1756) Winchester World Standard Guns and Ammunition catalog and the July 1, 1940 Wholesale and Retail Price List listed the Model 61 (Miniature Target Boring) in .22 Long Rifle Shot at $21.75.

This gun had the 24 inch round barrel, the 17-groove forearm, and other features of the late variety 61 rifles with three exceptions: (1) it was bored for the .22 shot cartridge; (2) it had a number 81 front sight and no rear sight; (3) the receiver had a $\frac{5}{16}$ inch groove like Model 12's. Later receivers had smooth tops.

Early post World War II catalogs did not list the smooth bore. It was produced again in 1954 and the December 30, 1955 catalog listed it at $67.85. The 1940, 1955, and subsequent publications showed the same stock number, G6116R. The January 2, 1959 Wholesale-Retail Price List listed the smooth bore at $69.95. Subsequent publications did not show it. Production ceased in 1960 but some remained on hand until 1963.

According to Madis (1981, p. 239), 77 of these smoothbores were counter-bored $\frac{3}{8}$ inch diameter 10 inches back from the muzzle to reduce muzzle blast. Nine cased smoothbore Model 61 sets were assembled from 1937 to 1941.

Special Notes

1. It is doubtful that collectors will ever know how many smoothbore 61's were made. (The 61 was discontinued in 1963 at 342,001.)

2. There are rumors of rifle and smoothbore sets—two front sections for one butt section. I once wrote Winchester, asking whether they would fit a shot only section to my rifle. The reply said no and offered to replace the rifle barrel with a smoothbore.

3. The loading port in the magazine tube was shaped slightly differently from the port on rifles. Some of the butt sections were tapped for receiver sights as were some rifles—an anomoly of no great consequence.

4. Model 61's were used at Moskeet stands at fairs and carnivals. They were also used in commercial indoor clay target facilities around 1960. Winchester 61's and Remington 121's used in some of these facilities had Simmons ribs. Until I became a purist, I wanted one of those Model 61's with custom, checked wood to top off my Model 12 and Model 42 rack.

Model 67   1936–1948

The Model 67 was first listed in 1934. It was not available in .22 caliber shot until sometime after 1936. The .22 Long Shot and .22 Long Rifle Shot smoothbore was authorized on September 9,1936. Subsequent Winchester World Standard Guns and Ammunition catalogs did not list it. The 1938 price list listed it as $5.65. The July 1, 1940 Wholesale and Retail Price List listed the Model 67—Bolt Action Single Shot Rifle stock number G 6720 R—Smoothbore barrel for .22 Long Shot or .22 Long Rifle Shot cartridges at $5.45. This gun had the 75 C and 32 B sporting rifle sights.

The same catalog listed the Model 67—Stock number G 6716 R—.22 Long Rifle Shot (miniature target boring) 24″ barrel no. 81 front and 94 B middle sight at $8.98. This boring was authorized on April 24, 1940. It was bored approximately ⅜ inch, from the muzzle to a depth of approximately 12 inches.

Both guns had the late shotgun style stock without finger grooves and 27 inch round, tapered barrels. They weighed approximately 5¼ pounds—¼ pound more than rifles. They were not serially marked.

The October 1, 1946 Retail Price List listed the G 6720R gun at $12.85. The 1948 and subsequent publications did not. Production ceased in 1949. It is likely that this gun was available for only a year or so before WW II and survived only three years after WW II. It is unlikely that collectors will ever know how many were made.

Special Notes

1. The .22 Long Rifle Shot cartridge contains only 25 grains of No. 12 shot. It is difficult to break a clay target with so little striking power. At best these were snake and rat guns. They sufficed for sparrows and other pests in confined quarters such as chicken houses. They would also sting dogs and cats. None of these uses is recommended for humane reasons. Shot cartridges in centerfire pistol calibers are much more effective.

2. A complete collection of Winchester shotgun variations would contain four .22 Long Rifle Shot arms: one Model 61 with grooved receiver, a Model 61 with smooth receiver, a Model 67 with rifle sights and the small bore, and a Model 67 with a shotgun sight and the large bore.

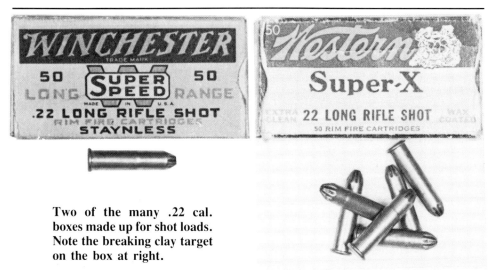

**Two of the many .22 cal.
boxes made up for shot loads.
Note the breaking clay target
on the box at right.**

Chapter 11

MODEL 42

Probably no Winchester model was so universally loved and so little used as the Model 42. Almost no one who owned a 42 said anything bad about it. Skeet shooters, a few quail hunters and ladies and juniors used them extensively. Only 159,353 were made.

John M. Olin played a major role in the introduction of the Model 42. The gun was originally designed for the 2½ inch shell and was nearly ready for production in late 1932, but Mr. Olin had introduced the Super-X heavy game load and because of its success insisted that the new gun be made for three inch shells. Because this required a new design, the first 42's were delivered to the warehouse in May 1933. It was announced in the August 12, 1933 price list.

Catalog no. 89, 1934, was the first to describe 42's.

The new Model 42 Winchester Slide Action Hammerless .410 Repeater is of completely new design and construction. It has a general similarity in appearance to the famous Model 12 Winchester, but in each and every part, it is a .410 shotgun. Model 42 is the first American made .410 repeater to handle a 3 inch shell and the first pump action gun designed for such a shell. This chambering for 3 inch shells makes the Model 42 a unique achievement in American gun making.

Model 42 is made in two styles, the Standard Grade gun and the Model 42 Skeet Gun. Both styles are chambered expressly for 3″ shells, but in addition will also handle the regular 2½″ 410 gauge shell.

The Standard Grade is furnished with either 26″ or 28″ full choke, modified choke or cylinder bore barrel of Winchester Proof Steel, pistol grip walnut stock, hard rubber butt plate and round slide handle with circular grooves. The Skeet Gun is furnished with 26 inch Skeet Choke Barrel of Winchester Proof Steel, straight grip walnut stock, checkered, hard rubber butt plate, and extension action slide handle, checkered. The magazine of each gun has a capacity of five 3 inch shells or six 2½ inch shells.

You have in this new Winchester not only a light, entirely new designed and built man-sized six-shot repeater, but a gun that with its new Winchester 3 inch Repeater Super Speed 410 gauge shell actually doubles the usual 410-gauge performance—a gun actually putting double the usual number of shot in a 20 inch circle at 30 yards—patterning more than the entire charge of other 410-gauge guns. With this 3 inch shell, the Model 42 equals the performance of a 28 gauge gun, and in fact is not far behind the performance expected from 20 gauge guns a few years ago. The 3 inch shell is conspicuously imprinted on the body, marking it for the 3 inch chamber only.

Model 42 will prove ideal for the wide variety of sport which hand trap shooting provides, in addition to its fine service for field and skeet shooting. With the rapidly increasing popularity of Skeet and the inclusion of .410 events in all of the big Skeet Tournaments, the Model 42 now places every shooter in a position to own a hammerless, take down, six shot .410 repeater.

This new Winchester handles exquisitely. It is excellently balanced, light in weight, and beautiful in its line. It has a racy appearance and will appeal to every lover of fine guns as in every respect a thoroughbred. The Standard Grade gun with 26″ barrel weighs 5⅞ pounds and with 28″ barrel 6 pounds. The Model 42 Skeet Gun weighs 6 pounds.

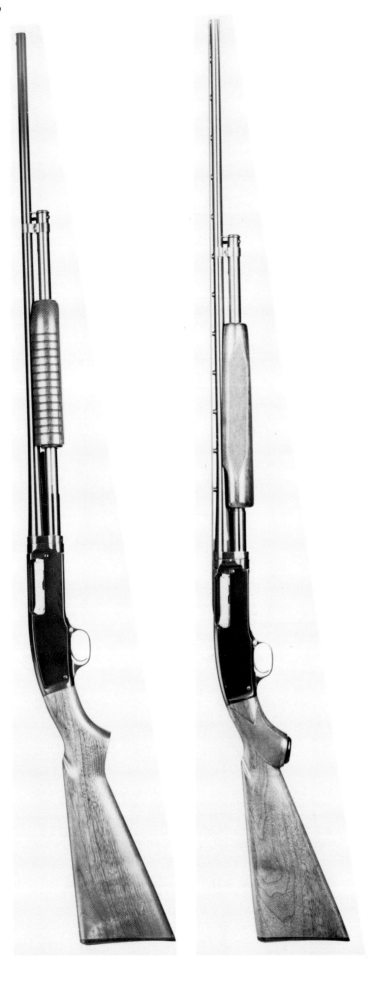

From left—Field Grade no. 125XXX, .410 bore, 26″. This is a late gun.

Skeet Gun no. 148XXX, .410 bore, 28″. This late gun has the Winchester Special Ventilated Rib and steel grip cap.

Another distinctive feature of the Model 42 is the special Winchester Skeet Choke boring which has been developed and is standard on the Skeet Gun. Barrels with this Skeet boring can also be had, if so specified, on the Model 42 Standard Grade gun. This boring delivers remarkably effective and consistent patterns for skeet shooting which places this gun in a class by itself for small gauge skeet shooting. In addition, the Skeet Choke is admirably adapted to small gauge upland shooting.

Perhaps "exquisite" and "racy" were well chosen words. The 1934 Winchester World Standard Guns and Ammunition catalog (WWSG&A) made note of the facts that at the end of the 1933 season the 42 held the 410 bore long run world's record at skeet—more than double the previous record—and that it had started the 1934 season by taking the Florida All Gauge Championship.

Standard or Field Grade 1933–1963

Catalog no. 89 listed standard grade guns with 26 and 28 inch barrels with full, modified, and cylinder bore and 26 inch skeet choke. Plain and matted rib barrels were available. The 28 inch barrels with skeet chokes could be special ordered. Over the years, the barrel lengths and choke and plain barrel/matted rib combinations were gradually reduced. For a time after 1954, field guns could be special ordered with Winchester Special Ventilated Ribs. The 1959 catalog listed only 26 inch full, modified, or improved cylinder and 28 inch full choke plain barrels.

The 1960 catalog listed only 26″ full and modified plain barrels. On June 27, 1945 a larger standard slide handle was authorized. This slide handle was almost flat on the bottom and grooved on the sides. It was introduced in 1947. The shape of pistol grips was altered as it was on other models. The last field guns had full pistol grips with a large flat bottom. The 1962 catalog listed the field gun at $109.00.

Trap Grade 1934–1939

This gun was furnished with checked fancy pistol grip stock and small forearm and 26 inch full choke. Extras at no additional charge were 28 inch barrel, any of the standard chokes, straight or pistol grip stock of special dimensions, Winchester or any rubber recoil pad listed in the catalog, and middle sights on solid ribs. Extension slide handles and interchangeable barrel assemblies were available at extra charge.

The 1939 WWSG&A showed this gun but DISCONTINUED was overprinted in red.

Skeet Gun 1934–1963

The first skeet grade guns had straight grips and checked extension slide handles, plain or raised matted rib barrels, 3 inch chambers, and 26 inch skeet choked barrels. The 1934–1938 WWSG&A's listed full, and modified chokes and cylinder bore in 26 and 28 inch. The 1939 WWSG&A did not list 28 inch barrels. It did list optional pistol or straight grip stocks and 2½ inch chambers on special order. Subsequently 2½ inch chambers were optional. The pistol grip was authorized on June 28, 1939 and became standard on May 6, 1940. The 1948 catalog listed only 28 inch guns with plain or matted rib barrels. By 1950, only 28 inch matted rib barrels were available.

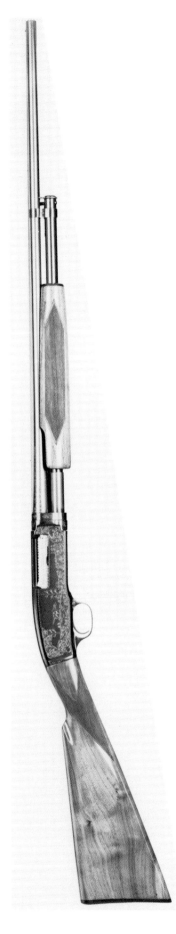

Appendix B is a flyer which introduced the Winchester Special Ventilated Rib on Skeet, Deluxe, and Field Model 42's. The January 2, 1954 retail price list did not show matted rib guns. In all six barrels were available: 2½ or 3 inch chambers with matted ribs, or Winchester Special Ventilated Ribs, or Winchester Special Ventilated Ribs and steel Cutts Compensators. The December 30, 1955 and subsequent retail price lists did not show the 2½ inch chamber with Cutts Compensator. The 1960 catalog listed only the 3 inch chamber 28 inch Winchester Special Ventilated Rib Barrel with skeet choke. The 1962 catalog listed this gun at $180.00.

Skeet Gun—Trap Grade 1934–1939

This gun had straight grip fancy walnut stocks and extension slide handles with two unchecked diamond-shaped areas in the side checking panels as did the later deluxe grade guns. Barrels were plain or with raised matted ribs, 3 inch chambers, and skeet chokes. The no-charge extras which were available on trap grade guns were also available on this gun.

The 1934 and subsequent WWSG&A's did not show this gun separately. Through 1939, they noted that the skeet gun could also be had in trap grade. The advantage of trap grade was higher quality walnut and butt stock dimensions to order.

De Luxe 1950?–1963

The literature does not tell when this gun was introduced. The 1950 Wholesale-Retail Price List and General Catalog effective December 15, 1950 may have been the first listing. The De Luxe was comparable to pigeon grade Model 12's and 50's. This gun had full fancy walnut, fancy checking with one unchecked diamond-shaped area on the side of the grip and two on the side of the slide handle, hand smoothed working parts, and engine turned breech bolt and carrier. It was made on special order only to customer dimensions, with cheek piece, Monte Carlo or offset at extra charge. The February 2, 1950 Distribuor Catalog indicated that Model 42's could be engraved in the standard styles or much more elaborately. This rare catalog pictured a gun which made 42-5 engraving look very plain. Distributors were apprised that elaborately engraved, gold or silver inlaid 42's were fine presentation guns. Such a present!

The Winchester Special Ventilated Rib was introduced in 1954. Chamber, choke, and rib option declined as they did on field and skeet guns.

The 1962 catalog listed this gun at $280.00.

Special Notes

1. The Model 42 was especially well suited to embellishment. Engraving and carving paralleled what is available for Model 12's. Engraving was designated 42-1, 42-1A, 42-1B, 42-1C, 42-2, 42-3, 42-4, or 42-5. Styles which featured waterfowl on Model 12's featured "upland scenes and other appropriate subjects to conform to the purposes for which Model 42 is designed." Carvings 42-A and 42-B were comparable to fancy checking on Model 12's. Gold or silver inlays could be ordered.

2. Skeet and deluxe guns with pistol grips had the hard rubber grip cap (same as found on Model 12's) and later the first variety metal cap.

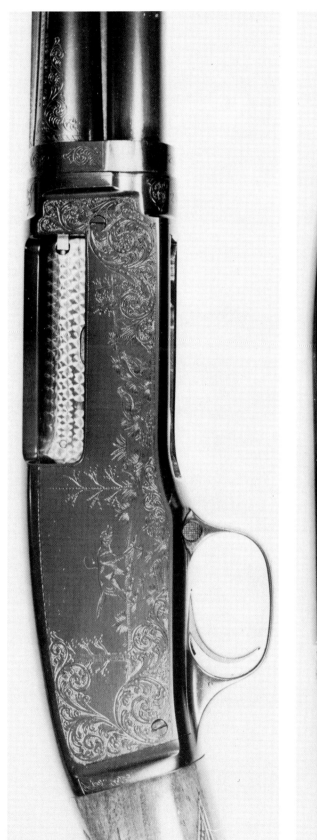

Engraving detail on .410 bore, 26" Skeet Gun no. 29XXX illustrated on previous page. This specimen has the straight grip, solid rib, factory 42-5 engraving. An instant favorite of most who handle it.

3. Mechanical parts did not change. Chamber length, ribs, and the Cutts Compensator were the only changes to the metal.

4. According to Barnes et al., (1980) Winchester did not install ventilated ribs on Model 42's. According to Simmons (1982), Winchester Special Ventilated Ribs were installed by Simmons on Model 42's which were returned to New Haven in the white. Simmons believed that Winchester did not install any ribs on Model 42's itself. Grant Tom stated that men at the factory installed ventilated ribs on one or two Model 42's. Like those on Model 12's, Model 42 ventilated ribs had two diameter or cylindrical posts, either squiggly lines north and south and east and west or straight lines, and either Simmons trademarks or no trademarks. Appendix B describes guns available with Winchester Special Ventilated Ribs on regular and special order. Catalogs from 1954 through 1960 showed the Winchester Special Ventilated Rib. The 1961 and 1962 catalogs showed the same guns but did not use the term Winchester Special Ventilated Rib.

5. Few 42's were used long and hard enough to require repairs. Many guns used for skeet passed from shooter to shooter, seeing double or triple duty. Some gunsmiths reported that left hand extractors broke repeatedly. Any 42 which was used a lot had a shiny magazine tube and receiver extension. The action slide handle metal was of two-piece construction and subject to looseness. Thus, it rubbed bluing much worse than did comparable parts on Model 12's. This was the major failing of the 42. It was remarkably reliable and easy to operate.

Ducks on a .410 box do not seem right. The white label is printed with blue and red.

Speed Loads were a big improvement for the .410 but still not adequate for ducks or other larger game birds. Most hunters used 3″ shells in the Model 42. The label at right is cream with red and blue print.

Chapter 12
MODEL 37

In 1936 Winchester introduced a single shot shotgun which was a major departure from its cast-iron framed competitors. The Model 37 made use of deep-draw steel forming and copper brazing processes, which were developed in the automotive industry. The 1936 World Standard Guns and Ammunition was quite realistic.

> To meet the growing demand for a strong, quick-operating single-shot Winchester shotgun, shooting all standard ammunition, at a price comparable to that of an ordinary .22 rim fire rifle, Winchester has developed an altogether new gunbuilding method for the production of its new Steelbilt Model 37. This new Winchester is made with steel in all metal parts—exceedingly tough, selected steel. Its frame is of an ingenious new Winchester design—super strong—with corresponding ingenuity and strength in bolting, lock construction and assembly with the super-strong steel barrel. The all-steel bolting parts and forged barrel lug are doubly large. Action, top-lever breakdown with pivot bolting. Semi-hammerless lock with low safety cocking lever located well forward on tang. Double-action automatic ejection, starts shell extraction by positive mechanical force as gun is opened and ejects by spring power. Genuine American walnut stock with pistol grip and composition butt plate; dimensions 14″ × 1½″ × 2¼″. Large, full, rounded fore-end, same diameter entire length, fits any reach. Winchester proof-marked steel barrel is full choke, giving approximately 70% pattern. Barrel lengths: 12, 16 and 20 gauges, 32″, 30″ or 28″; 28 gauge, 30″ or 28″; 410 gauge, 28″ or 26″. Chambered for 2¾ inch shells in 12, 16, and 20 gauges, 2⅞″ in 28 gauge and 3″ in 410, shooting all standard loads. Single shot. Weight in 12 gauge with 30″ barrel, approximately 6½ lbs. Take down.

The first guns were delivered to the warehouse on February 10, 1936. The .410 bore guns were likely not available until late 1936 or early 1937. The Model 37 was offered for a long time with few modifications. The December 15, 1950 Wholesale-Retail Price List listed only the 12 gauge in 30 inch full choke, and the 16, 20, and 410 in 28 inch full choke, with a footnote indicating that no other gauges, barrel lengths, or chokes would be provided. The 32 inch 12 gauge and 26 inch 410 were listed in the January 2, 1954 catalog. (It is likely that other than full chokes could be special ordered at some times prior to 1950.)

Model 37 Beginners Single Shot Shotgun 1958–1963

The January 2, 1958 catalog listed this 20 gauge gun with 26″ modified choke at $31.95. It had the solid red recoil pad.

Model 37's were not serially marked. This model was discontinued in 1963 at approximately 1,015,554. Gauge/barrel length combinations diminished even further during the last several years.

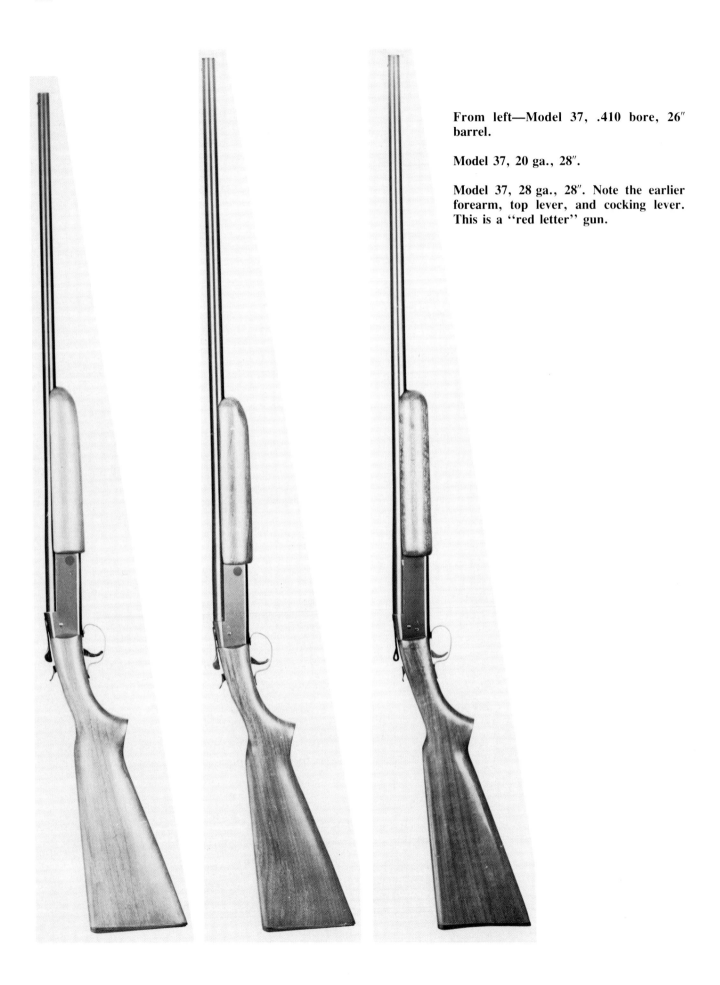

From left—Model 37, .410 bore, 26″ barrel.

Model 37, 20 ga., 28″.

Model 37, 28 ga., 28″. Note the earlier forearm, top lever, and cocking lever. This is a "red letter" gun.

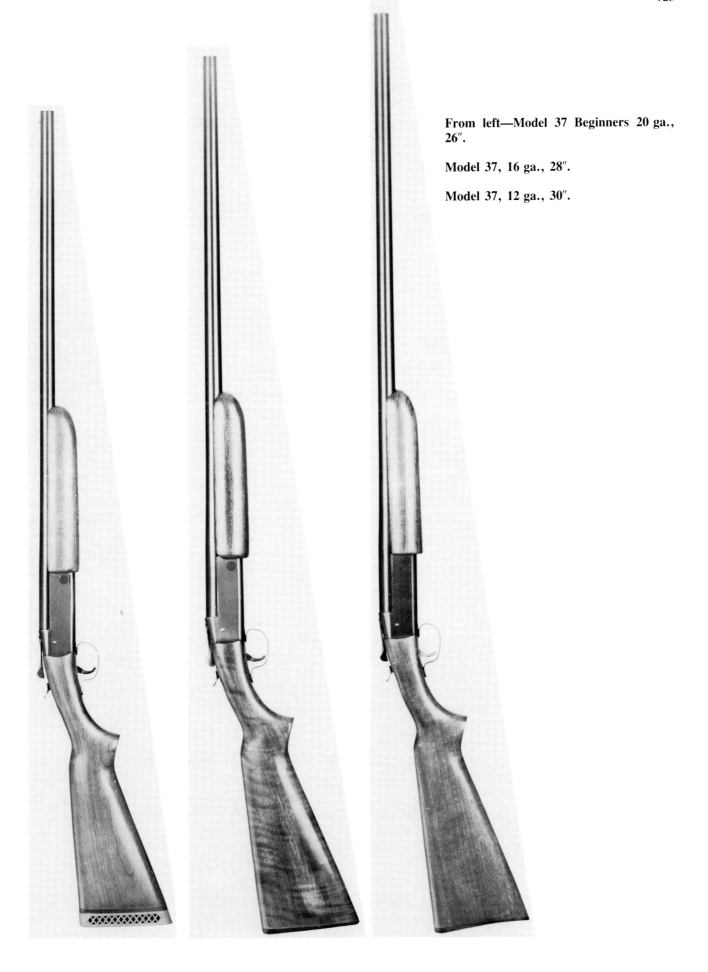

From left—Model 37 Beginners 20 ga., 26″.

Model 37, 16 ga., 28″.

Model 37, 12 ga., 30″.

Special Notes

1. Several changes occurred. An export style forearm was authorized on March 22, 1936. This forearm was not quite as large as the first forearm and it was more rounded at the front. This style was authorized for all 37's on December 4, 1941. Combs on later guns were shorter at the front and not as pointed as on early guns.

2. The first top levers were formed from sheet metal. At the rear, the metal was folded, leaving a tear-shaped hole. A forging was authorized on September 25, 1936. The new top lever was much more attractive.

3. The first receivers had Winchester stamped under the receiver. The depressed logo was painted red—thus red letter 37's, which many collectors prefer. After approximately 1948, receiver bottoms were plain.

4. The first cocking levers were gracefully shaped and little more than one eighth inch wide. A similarly shaped but wider cocking lever was later introduced. Finally, a concave, spade-shaped cocking lever which was even wider was authorized on February 19, 1937. This was properly called a cocking lever because it served to pull the striker into cocked position (and did not itself strike a firing pin). The lock spring guide was reshaped to make for an easier trigger pull.

5. As on many other models, the early butt plate had the round logo and the later one had the vertical Winchester logo. Barrel markings were changed several times.

6. John M. Olin affected the Model 37 in at least one way. So that he and guests at Nilo Farms, Georgia might have snake protection, Mr. Olin had a number of 410 gauge Model 37's made up into legal length pistols; that is, 18 inch or slightly longer barrels and 26 inch or slightly longer overall. Estimates of number made are 24 to 30. The one which I examined had a nicely crowned muzzle and had been sawed off at the pistol grip. Metal and wood were finished as were other 37's, and the forearm and grip had coarse checking in keeping with that found on other shotguns of the era, i.e., appearing to be factory. High level Olin employees have been quick to say that these and other special items were made up at Mr. Olin's behest.

7. From several sources, I have heard that a few Model 37's were made for 8 gauge industrial shells. Perhaps fifteen were made in the 1930's for an aluminum company in Alabama. One wonders whether 8 gauge barrels could be seated low enough in 12 gauge actions to center primers on the firing pin. Likely the action or firing pin or both had to be altered to accommodate the longer radius.

8. There are also reports that a few Model 37's were made up in .45–70. Anything more would be more than I know about this matter. It would be a simple matter to line Model 37 barrels for all but extremely large calibers. But, for whom, for what, when?

9. A Model 38 shotgun was authorized on November 18, 1936. Only sample guns were made up. This gun was a true hammerless model with a tang safety. It was not offered for sale.

10. The Model 37 was a fine shotgun for its intended use. It was stout and reliable. It was the only regularly supplied gun made by Winchester in five gauges. (Counting magnum 12's and 20's, the 21 was offered in seven chamberings, but all 410's were custom built.) A collection of 37's should include the five standard guns and the beginner's gun. One can be proud to have all five gauges in very good or better condition and with red letters. The 28 gauge changes hands so rarely that one cannot price it. A great many gunners would not part with the Model 37 with which they started hunting.

Wonder shells were offered for a short time in 1920. There were green 12 and 16 gauge empties, yellow 12 gauge empties, green 12 gauge loaded shells, and likely 16 gauge loaded shells. Notice the huge battery cup primer. This is among the rarest of Winchester shells. The box label from a brochure in Spanish is red. Little is known about Winco shells. They are very much like Wonders, though the battery cup primer is smaller. The one here is a factory load.

The red NIMROD shell illustrated below was made for export and sold to the Normal Powder Company of England as a primed empty. Similar shells were made by Union Metallic Cartridge Company for Normal but these have a case wall imprint and U.M.C. headstamp. Specimen in Guenter Wienert collection.

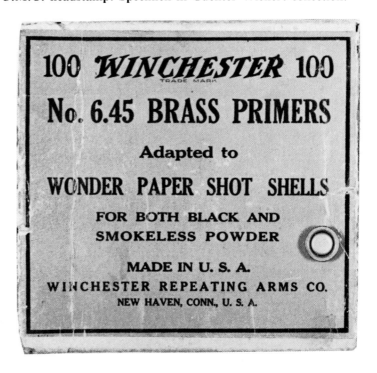

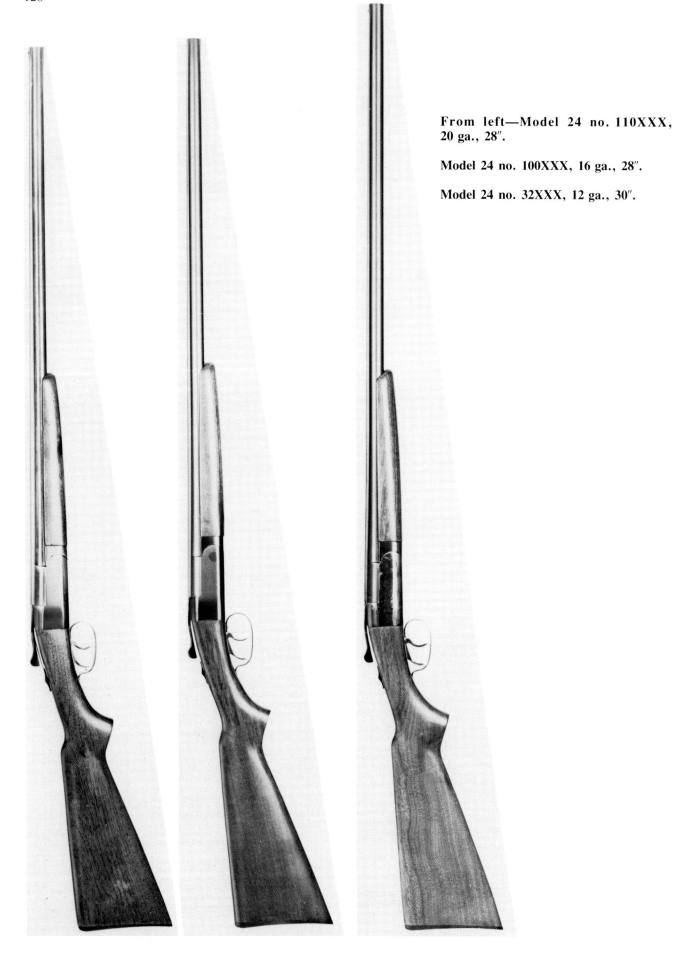

From left—Model 24 no. 110XXX, 20 ga., 28″.

Model 24 no. 100XXX, 16 ga., 28″.

Model 24 no. 32XXX, 12 ga., 30″.

Chapter 13

MODEL 24

The Model 24 employed many of the design and production features of the Model 37. For example, the Model 24 had a very long hinge pin. The first guns were delivered to the warehouse on April 21, 1939. The 1939 World Standard Guns and Ammunition introduced the gun. The description of the 16 and 20 gauge guns in the next issue (undated from no. 1756) was more thorough.

> With new modern streamline styling, Model 24 is the latest in standard double-barrel hammerless shotgun design. Built to sell at a very moderate price, a distinct new contribution to the long era of double-barrel hammerless shotgun popularity, it is a remarkable value. A surprisingly nice handling, finely balanced, hard shooting gun, for the shooter who has his heart set on a finely styled double gun yet must buy in the moderate-priced bracket. Receiver, barrels and all important parts are made of high-grade steel. There are no castings anywhere. Frame is machined from a solid steel forging, and extra strong. Extra strength is carried out in the action design, combining locking bolt, barrel lug, hinge pin, forearm shoe, and forearm lug. Barrels fit down deep and snugly in the receiver, giving the whole gun breech an especially attractive rounded contour. Locking bolt, barrel lug and hinge pin are wide and sturdy, with large bearing surfaces. Lug fits snugly in a deep recess in the receiver. Bolting is exceptionally strong, simple, dependable. Firing action is exceedingly fast. Barrels are of Winchester selected steel, with matted rib: 12 ga., 30″, 28″ or 26″; 16 ga. and 20 ga., 28″ or 26″. Extractors, cam operated, with supplemental spring action. Stock is genuine American walnut, with full-rounded low, streamlined comb and full pistol grip; streamlined to receiver. Dimensions: 14½″ × 1½″ × 2½″, with 2″ down pitch. Streamlined semi-beavertail forearm of matching walnut, shaped to the barrels, coming up high at the sides, and accurately fitted. Automatic safety. Take down. Weight approximately 7½ lbs.

All of the above was true!

The 16 and 20 gauge guns were introduced in 1940. They were made on one size frame. Both 30 and 28 inch 12 gauge barrels were bored modified and full. Initially 12 gauge 28 and 26 inch and 16 and 20 gauge 26 inch barrels were bored cylinder and modified. In 1947, cylinder boring was changed to improved modified. The guns weighed approximately 7 lbs. 7 oz., 6 lbs. 9 oz., and 6 lbs. 8 oz. respectively.

Straight grip stocks could be ordered at no extra charge. Perhaps better walnut, checked or not, and special dimensions could be special ordered at extra cost. However, I have never heard of such a fancy finished Model 24. There have been rumors of Model 24's with automatic ejectors. People probably mistake the separate extractors for ejectors because on other side-by-sides, extractors are one-piece. Serial number 2 was an experimental gun with single selective trigger and automatic ejectors.

The Model 24 was a very good gun. Yet, it had limited appeal, likely because World War II emphasized automatic fire.

The 1956 price list showed all of the original gauge/barrel length/choke combinations. The 1957 price list showed none, but some remained on hand until 1958. Approximately 116,280 were made.

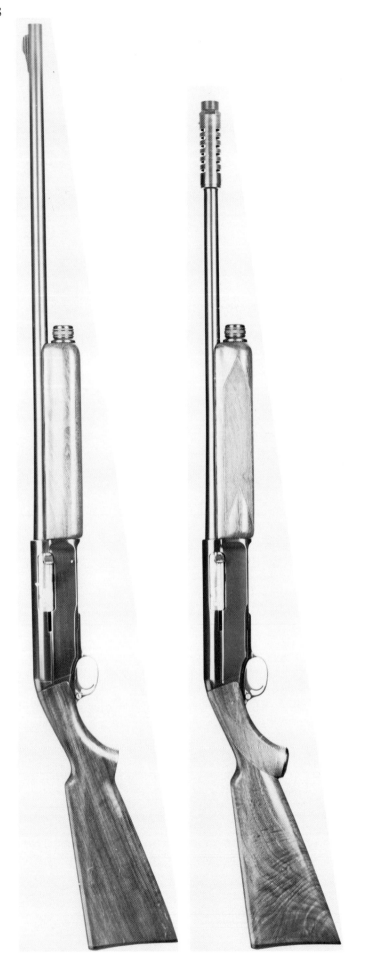

Left—Field gun no. 34XX, 12 ga., 30″.

Skeet gun no. 24XX, 12 ga., 24″ over spreader tube. An unfired specimen.

Chapter 14

MODEL 40

The January 2, 1940 price list introduced Winchester's second self-loading, long recoil shotgun. The Model 40 was designed on demand of John M. Olin and was intended to compete with self-loaders such as Browning and Remington which were popular in the field and on skeet ranges. It was the first self-loader with smooth-curved receiver back. The first guns were delivered to the warehouse in January 1940.

Field Gun 12 Gauge 1940–1941

The July 1, 1940 price list was one of very few pieces of literature which described the Model 40. The field gun was listed at $52.42.

> This handsomely streamlined completely new design Model 40 represents the latest development of the Winchester Automatic (Self-loading) gun principle. It includes a number of new features that combine to make it the outstanding gun of its type of smoothness of operation, balance and handling feel and mechanical precision.
>
> Model 40 is made to the following specifications: Pistol grip stock of Standard grade American walnut. Stock and forearm not checked. Dimensions: Length of pull 14″; Drop at comb, 1½″; Drop at heel, 2½″; Pitch down, 2″.
>
> Stock to customer's special dimensions can be furnished at extra charge on special order only.

Straight grip stocks could be special ordered without charge. All model 40's had hard rubber butt plates.

Plain barrels only were provided, and sight ramp and bead were forged integral with the barrel. Standard lengths/chokes were 30 or 28 inch full or modified. The magazine held four shells. This gun weighed approximately eight pounds and was 51½ inches long with a 30 inch barrel.

Skeet Gun 1940–41

All skeet guns were furnished with Cutts Compensators. They were listed at $78.30. The July 1, 1940 price list was terse.

> Pistol grip stock and forearm of American walnut, checkered. Rubber pistol grip cap.
>
> Stock dimensions: Length of pull; 14″; Drop at comb, 1½″; Drop at heel, 2½″; Pitch down, 2″.
>
> Special plain unchoked barrel with shoulder forged on muzzle end, threaded to fit the threading on compensator body. Neither solid raised matted rib nor ventilated rib barrels can be furnished.

Compensator is Lyman Style A set with Cutts Compensator body, two choke tubes (one a spreader for Skeet, and one .705 full choke) and a special wrench for attaching or removing tubes. Modified choke tube can be substituted for full choke, if so ordered, without extra charge.

Skeet guns weighed approximately 8 lbs., 4 oz. Compensator bodies were steel, bright aluminum, or blackened aluminum. Straight grip stocks could be special ordered without charge. Straight or pistol grip stocks with special dimensions could be special ordered at extra charge.

Special Notes

1. Skeet guns were first demonstrated at a skeet shoot in Tucson, Arizona in 1938. Afterwards, Mr. Olin asked a high level production employee what he thought of the gun. The employee warned Mr. Olin that he would not like the reply. Urged to go on, he replied that the Model 40 was not worthy of the Winchester name because it was unsafe and had inherent weaknesses and design faults. Nevertheless, the Model 40 was further developed and introduced to the trade. An elm insert was placed near the rear of forearms after serial number 1172. Although it is reported that only 12,000 were made, I have it from a Winchester employee that from design models through final discontinuance and parts clean up during World War II, on the order of 40,000 were manufactured—perhaps not all fully assembled and many scrapped because of serious faults.

2. Unlike other Winchester shotgun safeties, the Model 40 cross bolt safety was at the rear of the guardbow. The safety was unique in that it had a coin slot wihch facilitated turning it one fourth turn to lock it in the off position.

3. According to (Madis, p. 276) only 37 Model 40's were ordered with fancy, checked wood.

4. The 1945 catalog listed the Model 40. The 1946 catalog did not. The gun had been discontinued in 1941 and was not produced after World War II. Because of weaknesses, the Model 40 was recalled. One of the weaknesses was the magazine tube. It was not as sturdy as it might have been and was subject to being bent and thus preventing free motion of the barrel. Unbeknownst to many shooters the magazine tube bent downward, causing the gun to shoot low. Another weakness was timing. Internal parts could get so badly out of adjustment that the gun would fire before battery, i.e., before being fully closed. This was reason enough to recall Model 40's. Persons who returned Model 40's were sent Model 12's. Considering that the field grade was listed at $52.42, the skeet grade was listed at $78.30, and the comparable Model 12's were $43.64 and $71.24, people who returned Model 40's may have received added compensation.

The Model 40 certainly did not live up to the catalog verbage. Some operated smoothly most of the time. The gun was far from the epitome of balance and handling. Collectors will never know how many went under a trip hammer in New Haven. Rare is the collection which has unfired specimens of both grades of the most unsuccessful Winchester shotgun.

Chapter 15
MODEL 25

Winchester introduced this gun to compete with Remington and other slide action guns which were cheaper than the Model 12. The Model 25 could as well have been designated the solid-frame Model 12. The Model 25 was authorized on December 30, 1947 and the first guns were delivered to the warehouse on February 2, 1950. The December 15, 1950 price list was terse.

> The newest member of the Winchester family was introduced to meet a growing demand for a well-built, reliable, hammerless repeating shotgun with good handling qualities . . . at a popular price. All this has been accomplished in the Model 25. Its handsome appearance, smooth action, good balance and natural pointing qualities have already made this model popular with a host of sportsmen who want an all-around hard-shooting shotgun of traditional Winchester quality and craftsmanship. Made in 12-gauge only. Also furnished in riot gun style with 20″ cylinder bore barrel.

Field barrels were all 28 inch and choked either full, modified, or improved modified. The gun weighed approximately 7½ lbs. and was 47¼″ long. Stock dimensions were approximately 14″ × 1½″ × 2½″. The magazine held four shells. The 1954 catalog listed both field and riot guns, but 1955 and subsequent publications did not. Approximately 87,937 Model 25's were made.

Special Notes

1. Some Winchester users prefer Model 25's to Model 12's for field and home protection use because they seem to balance better and have the added feeling of security which only solid frame guns can provide.

2. Model 25's had no firing pin retractors. Some did not have cartridge guides and pivots.

3. Simmons Gun Specialties offered Model 25's with Simmons ventilated ribs. Occasionally, one sees a Model 25 made up with Model 12 or custom trap wood. Collectors should show interest only in plain guns because other than muzzle devices, the factory offered no options on Model 25's. Accept a Winchester solid recoil pad but nothing more.

Chapter 16

MODELS 50 AND 59

Model 50 1954–1961

The Model 50 was authorized on July 1, 1947. It was introduced in the January 2, 1954 price list and the first guns were sent to the warehouse on April 15, 1954. The Model 50 was revolutionary in two ways. (1) It was streamlined—unlike any previous autoloader. Literature bragged on the lack of screw heads and projecting pins. (2) It operated on the recoiling chamber principle. Its barrel remained stationary. The chamber moved back approximately one tenth inch, the bolt continued to the rear by inertia of itself and an inertia rod inside the stock, and the forward part of the cycle was powered by a spring inside the stock. The 1955 catalog boasted on the lack of "double shuffle" and the fact that one did not have to force the stock against the shoulder to make the action function.

> The all-new Winchester Model 50 Automatic shotgun works through an entirely different and revolutionary principle. When the Winchester Automatic is fired, the barrel remains stationary, fixed, rigid. The chamber moves back a fraction of an inch and starts the action on its way. Surely and smoothly, the Winchester easy-action Automatic flips out the empty and picks up a loaded shell, and you're ready for a really fast second shot. The easy, positive action of the Model 50 does its fast, smooth job every time, in spite of weather, weed-seeds or dirt.

The Model 50 was discontinued in December 1961. Approximately 196,402 were made, starting with number 1000 which was received by John M. Olin.

Field Gun 1954–1961: 12 and 20 Gauge

The January 2, 1954 price list showed only 12 gauge guns bored either 30 inch full, 28 inch modified, 26 inch improved cylinder, or 26 inch skeet. Full choke 28 inch barrels were listed in the January 24, 1955 price list. The May 7, 1954 special price list for Model 50's showed 20 gauge guns bored 28 inch full or modified and 26 inch improved cylinder or skeet. Field guns were first listed at $120.50. Winchester Special Ventilated Rib barrels, straight grips, and Monte Carlo or special dimension stocks were available at extra charge. The 1955 catalog noted that 20 gauge guns would be available in early 1956.

The January 2, 1958 catalog listed featherweight 12 gauge plain barrel and ventilated rib guns with all of the standard chokes. Featherweight guns had an "A" after serial numbers and "Featherweight" below the number. They were made with aluminum alloy receivers. A few mechanical parts were redesigned to reduce weight.

Skeet Gun 1954–1961: 12 and 20 Gauge

The January 2, 1954 price list showed only 26 inch 12 gauge guns with Winchester Special Ventilated Ribs and either skeet chokes or Cutts Com-

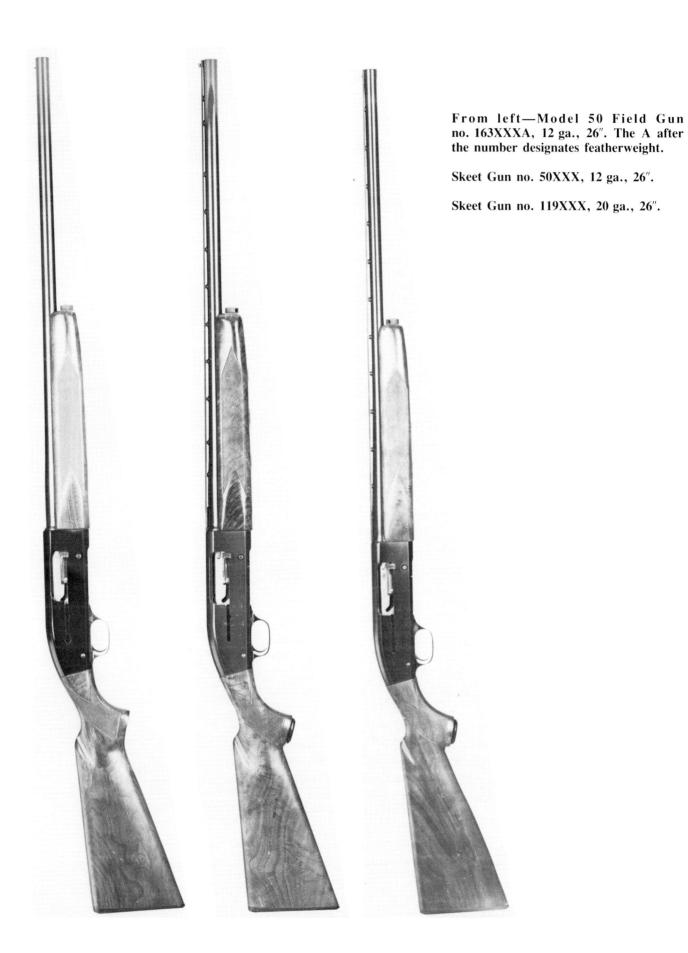

From left—Model 50 Field Gun no. 163XXXA, 12 ga., 26″. The A after the number designates featherweight.

Skeet Gun no. 50XXX, 12 ga., 26″.

Skeet Gun no. 119XXX, 20 ga., 26″.

pensators. The May 7, 1954 special price list for Model 50's showed 20 gauge guns with these same options. All the options available on field guns, even Monte Carlo stocks, were available at extra charge. The 1955 catalog noted that 20 gauge guns would be available in early 1956.

The January 2, 1958 catalog listed the 12 gauge featherweight gun. Several books indicate that 20 gauge featherweight skeet guns were supplied. Catalogs did not make clear that they were.

Trap Gun 1954–1961, 12 Gauge

The January 2, 1954 price list showed only 30 inch plain barrel, full choked guns. Winchester Special Ventilated Rib barrels and/or Monte Carlo stocks could be had at extra charge. The pictured gun had a hard rubber butt plate and the standard chamber. Perhaps a field gun was used for illustration because no trap gun was available for photographing. Thus, the first trap guns may be difficult to distinguish. Later trap guns had chambers with a projection at the top front of the ejection port which deflected spent shells downward. They had the solid red recoil pad. The May 7, 1954 special price list and subsequent literature showed only Monte Carlo guns with Winchester Special Ventilated Ribs. The same options were available at extra charge.

Pigeon Grade 1954–1961: 12 and 20 Gauge

The May 7, 1954 price list listed a large range of special order guns. As was the case with Model 12 pigeon and Model 42 deluxe guns, Model 50 pigeons had hand-honed interior parts and engine turned bolts and carriers. Any gauge and barrel length/choke combination offered in the lower grades could be ordered with stock dimensions to customer specifications. Pigeon guns had extra fancy walnut and larger checking panels. The regular extras, engraving and carving, and gold or silver inlays could be specified. Engraving and carving paralleled Model 12 ornamentation; that is, 50-1, 50-1A, 50-1B, 50-1C, 50-2, 50-3, 50-4, and 50-5 engraving and 50-A or 50-B carving. (These ornamentations were available on the lesser grades at least for a time.) PIGEON was stamped near the serial number.

The January 2, 1958 catalog listed featherweight field, skeet, and trap pigeon grade guns, apparently including 20 gauge field and skeet guns. The 1960 catalog made no mention of gauges, but it showed weights only for 12 gauge guns.

Special Notes

1. Buttstock checking was quite simple on field, skeet and trap guns, and only the sides of field forearms were checked. Trap and skeet guns had three diamonds under the forearm—two checked and one not. Skeet, trap, and pigeon guns had the first style steel grip cap. The hard rubber butt plate with round logo was replaced with the one with "Winchester" lengthwise during 1960.

2. The Model 50 was Winchester's third attempt to market an autoloader. Model 1911 and Model 40 guns totaled less than 95,000. In 50 years Winchester was not able to sell 300,000 autoloaders. (In the same period it sold over 1,900,000 Model 12's.) The major reason was likely poor reception of the Model 1911 (largely because it was opened unconventionally) and perhaps the poor

136

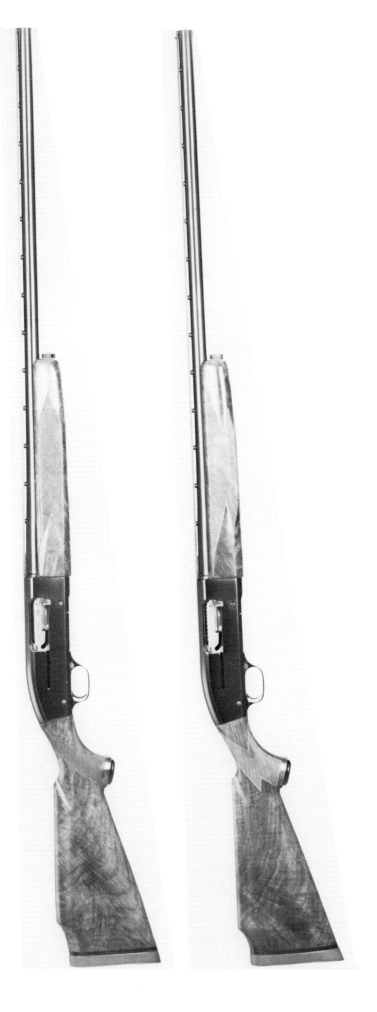

Left—Model 50 Trap Gun no. 117XXX, 12 ga., 30″, with Monte Carlo stock.

Pigeon Grade no. 58XXX, 12 ga., 30″, Monte Carlo.

balance of the Model 40. Obviously, gunners looked primarily to Browning and Remington for autoloaders and mostly to Winchester for slide actions (Remington running a distant second).

3. The Model 50 was reliable if the outside of the chamber was cleaned regularly and if the plunger which protruded from the rear of the chamber and assured that the chamber returned to battery was not lost. Standard weight guns were more durable than lightweight guns. (What else is new?)

4. Simmons Gun Specialties bored 12 and 20 gauge chambers so that they would shear off the front one fourth inch of three inch paper shells. They marked such chambers Simmons 3″ Chamber with an electric pencil. Standard weight guns with extra tension on the recoil spring withstood three inch shells rather well. Simmons did not advertise that it would convert featherweight guns. I have repaired two guns in which the action slides had worn and the action pin was bent from sustained use of three inch plastic shells. The conversion was for paper shells. Plastic 3 inch shells should not be used in any Model 50.

5. Simmons (1982) stated that Winchester installed ribs on all but proto type Model 50's. Simmons sold several design patents concerning the Model 50 to Winchester. Model 50's had the same post/rib top combinations as did Model 12's with Winchester Special Ventilated Ribs, i.e., two diameter and cylindrical posts with squiggly lines or straight lines on top. Simmons did not install ribs for Winchester on Model 50's. Thus, the purist will collect only guns with proof marks to the left of the rib and without Simmons trademarks.

6. Model 50's and 59's had many fine design features. Among the better features was the ejector. It was a long, durable rod, housed in the breech block. At the rear of the cycle, the breech block slid over it and the spent shell was ejected very positively. This system was simple and infinitely reliable because small, fragile parts were eliminated.

7. The hole through the receiver into the magazine tube was adequate for new shells and high quality reloads. Shells which had expanded head diameters because of repeated reloading often failed to leave the magazine. This condition could be alleviated by reaming the hole ten thousandths larger.

8. Serial number EXP33 was a 20 gauge Model 50 skeet with roll engraving. There were likely other experimental guns.

Model 59, 12 Gauge

The Model 59 was introduced in 1959 and first listed in the 1960 catalog. Advertising took note of the Win-Lite barrel, 6½ pounds, superior strength, weatherproof and other real and alleged features. It was billed as "The most significant advance in gun making techniques in more than 600 years." The brochure which announced the 59 was far from modest.

> Here is a most remarkable advance in the history of shotgun design and manufacture . . . the totally new Winchester Model 59 12-gauge, featuring the revolutionary, patented* Win-Lite barrel! Here's an entirely new thrill in shooting pleasure—with the fastest-firing autoloading shotgun on the market, combined with fast-swinging, perfect-pointing lightness that's a pleasure to carry through the toughest days in the field. The heart of the Model 59 lies in the unique Win-Lite barrel—an ingenious bonding of steel and glass fiber . . . finely polished and finished . . . the lightest, strongest shotgun barrel ever made! Ideally balanced by a super-strength ultra-light aluminum alloy receiver, the Winchester Model 69 has everything you want in a fine shotgun.
> NO POWER LOSS! The fixed barrel and floating chamber provide straight-line friction-free extraction and reloading with no loss of power in the system.

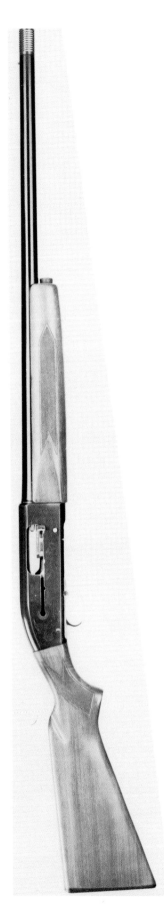

NON-RECOILING BARREL! This time and field-tested feature means you stay "on target" every time for a really fast second shot. No getting back on target as with some other autoloaders.

NO "DOUBLE SHUFFLE"! No forcing the shoulder into the stock to make the action work. The Model 59 action is smooth and unfailingly fast.

MAGNUM OR FIELD LOADS WITHOUT ADJUSTMENT! Shoots all 2¾" shells—regular field loads or super, long-range loads, including Magnum, without adjustment.

INSTANTLY INTERCHANGEABLE BARRELS! Change to any available Win-Lite barrel in seconds—anywhere, anytime—without tools.

20% LESS RECOIL EFFECT! A soft, steady push . . . not a sudden jab . . . with a measured 20% less recoil effect. Adds hours of shooting pleasure.

DAY-LONG CARRYING COMFORT! The ultra light weight of the Model 59 means more pleasant hours afield. Stay fresh, fast . . . and steady-on-target all day long!

WEATHER-PROOFED! Forget the weather! The outside surfaces of the barrel and receiver won't rust or corrode, regardless of temperature or weather conditions.

Surely the Win-Lite barrel was an innovation. It had a 20 thousandths thick steel liner and 500 miles of wound glass fiber. The rolled hunting scenes on the aluminum alloy receiver were firsts for Winchester. It was claimed that outside surfaces of the barrel and receiver could not rust or discolor. (Rust no. Discolor yes. Chamber areas of barrels turned yellow and receivers got white with sustained use.)

Standard Field Grade 1960–1965

The 1960 catalog listed 30, 28, and 26 inch Win-Lite barrels with full, modified, and improved cylinder chokes. A flyer listed both full and modified 28 inch barrels at $149.50. The 1961 catalog listed Winchester "Versalite" chokes. These were threaded into the barrel. Modified tubes were furnished and full and improved cylinder tubes could be had at $4.45. They had integral ventilated portions. A wrench, which was simply fashioned of sheet metal and stamped Winchester, was inserted through the vents to tighten or loosen the tubes. (Many gunners changed tubes without ever owning a wrench.) Only 26 inch barrels were fitted with Versalite chokes. The 1966 catalog did not list the Model 59.

Pigeon Grade 1962–1963

The pigeon gun was introduced in the 1962 catalog at $249.65. Like other pigeon or deluxe guns, it had custom wood made to customer specifications, hand-honed internal parts and engine turned bolts and carriers. The January 2, 1963 Winchester Rifles and Shotguns Wholesale-Retail Price List, showed plain barrel and Versalite choke pigeon guns with very fancy walnut, checking like Model 50 pigeons and the standard 59 game scenes. Evidently, engraving and carving were not available on 59's. The 1964 catalog did not list the pigeon grade.

Model 59 Field Grade no. 85XXX, 12 ga., 26". Winchester "Versatile" chokes and wrench were available with this model.

Special Notes

1. The Model 59 was one of the finest magazine guns ever made for upland game shooting. It is unfortunate that an honest, functional gun with modern material and design was not accepted by hunters. Only 82,085 were manufactured. But, many are still in use, especially in quail country. (The author and several of his quail hunting buddies use them for all feathered game.) One gunsmith buys good guns to disassemble for parts, which he ships all over the United States and Canada. The gun has more than a small following.

2. Early Model 59 forearms were shaped like Model 50 forearms. Later forearms were rather blunt-ended, i.e., less curved at the front. The 1962 Distributor Price List shows both forearms.

3. Most internal parts are the same as Model 50 parts. Several are the same as featherweight Model 50 parts. Win-Lite barrels can be used on Model 50 guns along with Model 59 forearms.

4. Many Model 59's were lightened by gunsmiths or hobbyists. Most have shortened and thinned forearms and carriers; some have drilled stocks and internal parts. It is wise to avoid mutilated guns.

5. A few Model 59's were made in 20 gauge, but little is known about these experimental guns. I do not know of one outside the factory. Several were made for 14 gauge all-aluminum shells, which were loaded by Western and Winchester.* Testing was done at Nilo Farms and near New Haven. According to Western and Winchester employees, the guns and ammunition functioned satisfactorily. However, the matter was not pursued because of the likely reluctance of gunners and the trade. Shells are quite common among shotshell collectors. At least 20 variations exist—Winchester vs. Western, roll vs. pie crimp, and various shot sizes. (Evidently, one or more Model 37's were also made for experimenting with these shells. One was listed in *Shotgun News* in 1981.)

This gauge was nominally successful in the early years of breech-loaders. Winchester sold new primed empty and factory loaded RIVAL paper shotshells and brass empties. Parker made a few 14 gauge doubles.

In 1949 District managers and salesmen were issued combination Winchester-Western sample cases. The two trays are almost identical. Salesmen were instructed to display the line which most appealed to the customer. Approximately 45 were distributed.

Trays are 15½ × 9½ inches (without the cover with logo) and the leather case which looks like a small briefcase is 16 × 10 × 4.

Chapter 17

HOW TO DESIGN A WINCHESTER SHOTGUN COLLECTION

There are many ways to design a Winchester shotgun collection. The obvious one for most collectors is to collect Model 12's and/or Model 21's. Similarly, one acquaintance collects only Model 97's. Some collect only Model 42's. Each of these four models can be a field in itself. One way to design a single model collection is to collect each of the grades or styles. This would be ten Model 97's—seven grades plus brush, riot, and trench guns. It would be at least 22 Model 12's—19 grades plus riot, trench, duck and Featherweight. There should be at least 12 Model 21's and six Model 42's. In all the other models, except the hammer doubles, it would be far fewer guns.

A much less obvious design is to collect all the models in each gauge. There were 22 models—not counting the Model 12 Featherweight separately. Across the 22 models, the total number of gauges was 40. To this should be added the Magnum Model 12 and the 12 and 20 gauge Model 21 magnums, bringing the total to 43. (Short and long chamber Model 41's and Model 42's would add two more. Short and long chamber 16 and 20 gauge chambers would add three more.) Forty-three seems the number of guns to collect to have all models in all gauges.

Not wanting to collect all the models, one could collect one or more action types. This design seems to interest rifle collectors more than shotgun collectors. All models and gauges in one or more action types would be interesting. In doubles it would be three hammer guns, seven Model 21's, and three Model 24's (13 total). In falling block it would be only the high wall. In lever it would be two Model 1887's and one Model 1901 (three total). In slide action there would be one Model 1893, two Model 1897's, five Model 12's, one Model 61, one Model 42, and one Model 25 (11 total). The cannon would be unique. In autoloader it would be one Model 1911, one Model 40, two Model 50's and one Model 59 (five total). In single shot break open, it would be one Model 20 and five Model 37's (six total). In bolt action it would be one Model 36, one Model 41 and one Model 67 (three total). Of course, the grand total of action types times gauges is 43 the same as for the models-time-gauges design.

Another design is to collect all the trap and skeet guns by gauge. At minimum, this would be two Model 1897's, one Model 1911, three Model 12's, one Model 21, one Model 42 and one Model 50 trap gun (nine total) *and* four Model 12's, five Model 21's, one Model 42, one Model 40, and two Model 50 skeet guns (13 total). This collection of 21 guns could be expanded by collecting all of the trap grade Model 97's and Model 12's and Model 21's; skeet, tournament, trap, custom, pigeon, and Grand American Model 21's; skeet, trap, and Deluxe Model 42's; and skeet and pigeon Model 40's. Obviously, this would be unattainable. But nine trap guns and 13 skeet guns would be attainable—if one could afford the small bore Model 21's and find a Model 40 skeet for sale.

I have always thought that a collection of one pigeon grade in each model would be admirable. This would be one each of Models 1897, 1911, 1912, 21,

50, and 59. Oddly, the most difficult to acquire would be the Model 59—the Model 1911 running a close second.

Even more interesting according to my tastes is a complete collection of riot and trench guns. This would be 10 and 12 gauge Model 1887's, solid frame riot and trench Model 97's, take down riot and trench Model 97's, riot and trench 12 gauge Model 12's, a riot 16 gauge Model 12, and a riot Model 25 (10 total). This design should include three Winchester manufactured 1917 Enfield bayonets. If it is established that Model 1893's were made up as riot guns, the total would be 11. These guns would not be especially expensive. But, assembling the full set might take a lifetime even without a quest for the rarest Model 12—the 16 gauge riot.

Perhaps the most intelligent design and almost certainly the best design from the standpoint of dollar appreciation would be to collect one of each model in the smallest gauge and highest grade or with highest embellishment available. This woule be a Match Gun 16 gauge hammer double, a high wall with fancy checked wood, a 12 gauge Model 1887 and a Model 1901 fancy finished, a Model 1893 with all the extras, a chromium plated cannon, a pigeon Model 1911, a 28 gauge pigeon Model 12 with number 5 engraving and B wood, a Model 20 with checked wood, a standard Model 36, a Model 41 with checked wood, a .410 bore Grand American Model 21, a standard Model 61, a standard Model 67, a Deluxe Model 42 with number 5 engraving, a .410 bore Model 37, a 20 gauge Model 24, a skeet Model 40, a standard Model 25, a 20 gauge pigeon Model 50 with number 5 engraving and B wood, and a pigeon Model 59. Like several of the other designs, this one might well take a lifetime to assemble even if money was no object. Several of these pieces might never come on the markct and even if each of them did, one collector would likely not read enough magazine advertisements, attend enough shows, or subscribe to enough lists to know that they were to be had.

Other designs should be considered. For example, a set of Model 12 pigeon guns with plain, matted, matted rib, and ventilated rib barrels would be unique. Lots of other possible designs come to mind. All the matted rib and/or all the ventilated rib guns is a big undertaking. One friend collects only 30 and 32 inch Model 12's. By gauge and grade and embellishment, this design has a lot of possibilities. Your design should be yours alone.

Collecting Winchester Shotguns is, in a word, intriguing.

WINCHESTER

Winchester guns were made not born.
The first from England with hammers and horn.
The rest from New Haven of steel and walnut mostly.
They showed how machines make good things less costly.
There were doubles—hammer & 21's & 24's.
There were levers—1887's & 1901's.
There were pumps—93's & 97's & 12's & 42's & 25's.
There were even breech loading cannons.
There were auto's—11's & 40's & 50's & 59's.
Thee were singles—20's & 36's & 41's & 37's.
There were rifle shotguns—high walls & 61's & 67's.
Most were for hunts and some were for warring.
Many were for targets and some were for policing.
No matter how used they were always the best.
No matter how old they outlasted the rest.

TIME LINE CHARTS

HAMMER DOUBLES

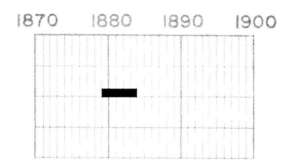

MODEL 1885 SINGLE SHOT

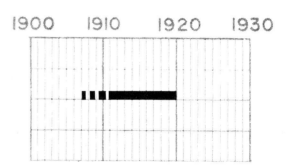

MODELS 1887 and 1901/01

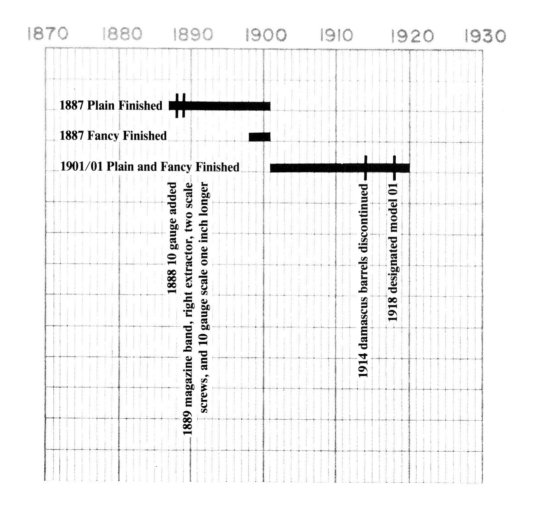

MODELS 1893 and 1897/97

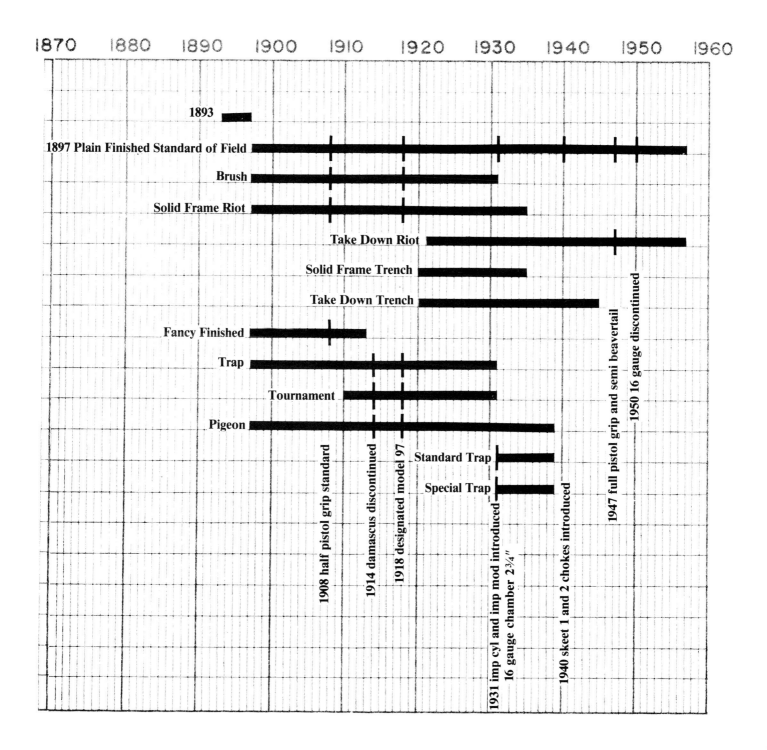

BREECH — LOADING CANNON

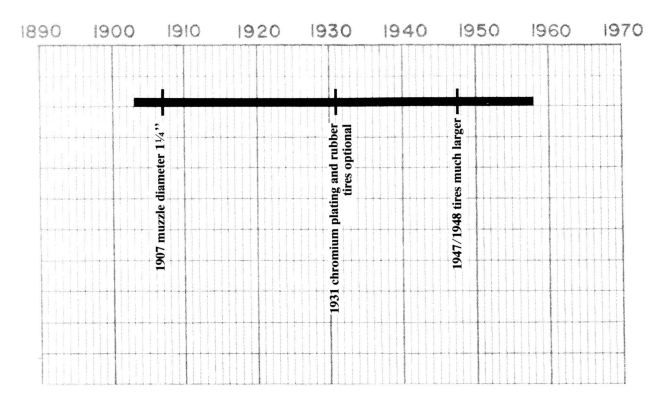

MODEL 1911/11

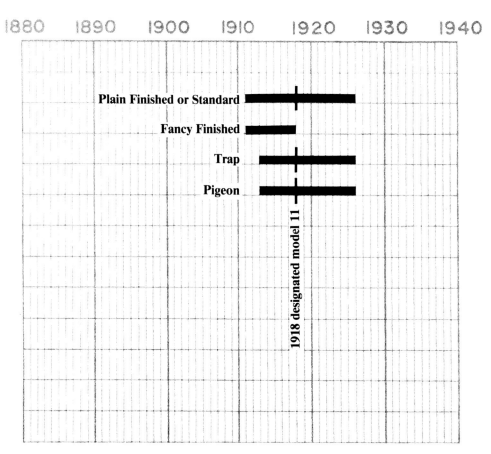

MODEL 1912/12

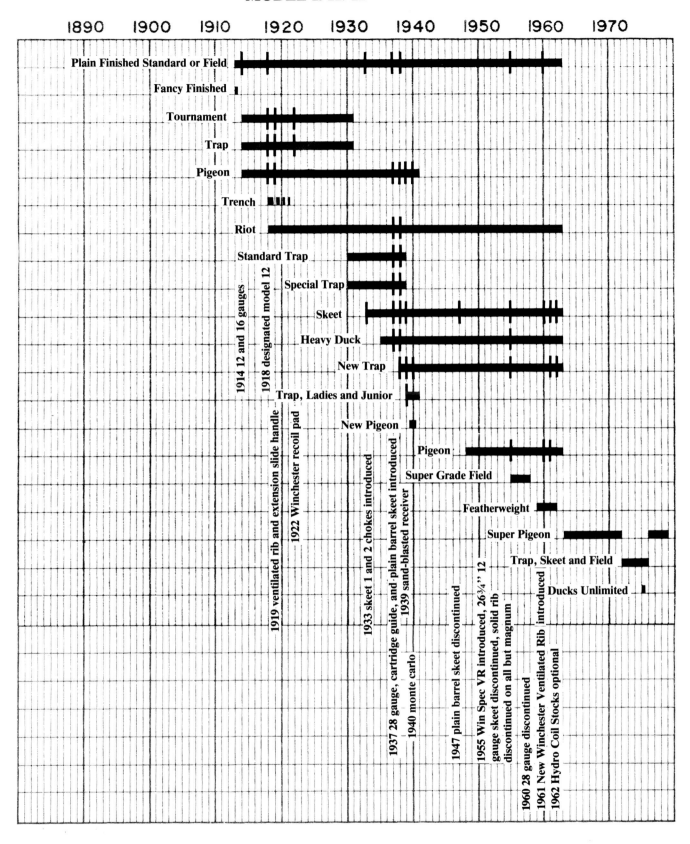

MODELS 20, 36, and 41

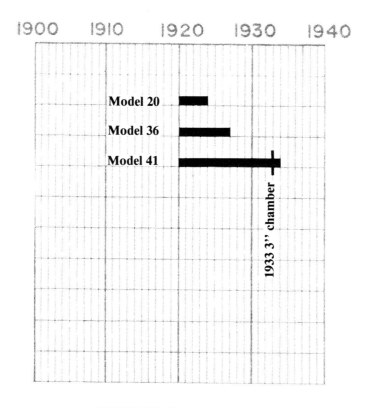

MODELS 61 and 67

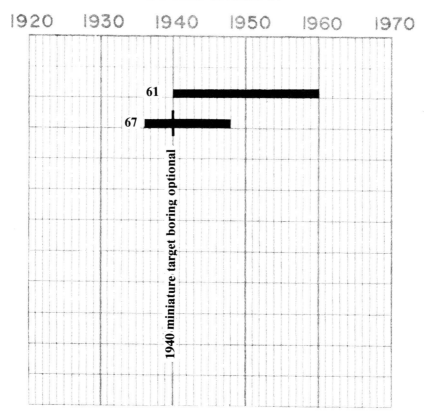

MODEL 21

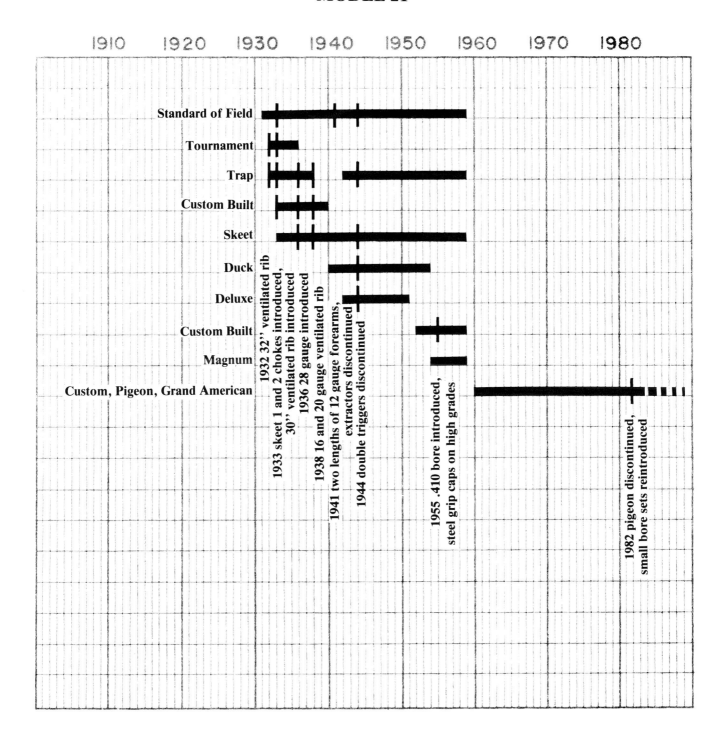

MODEL 42

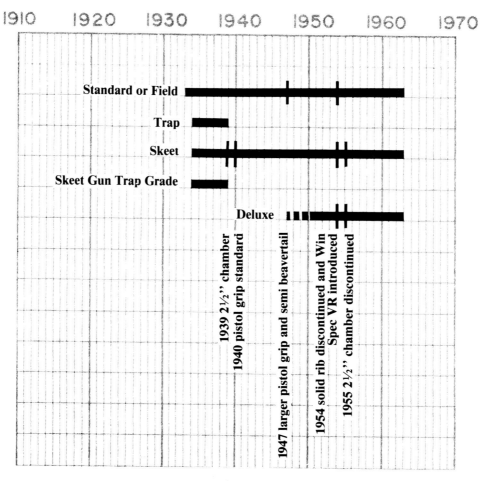

MODEL 37

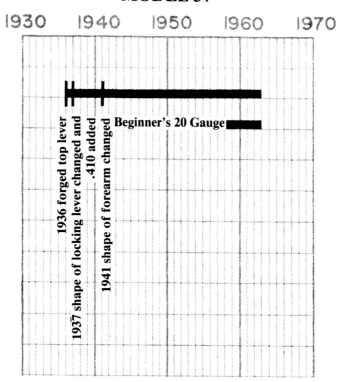

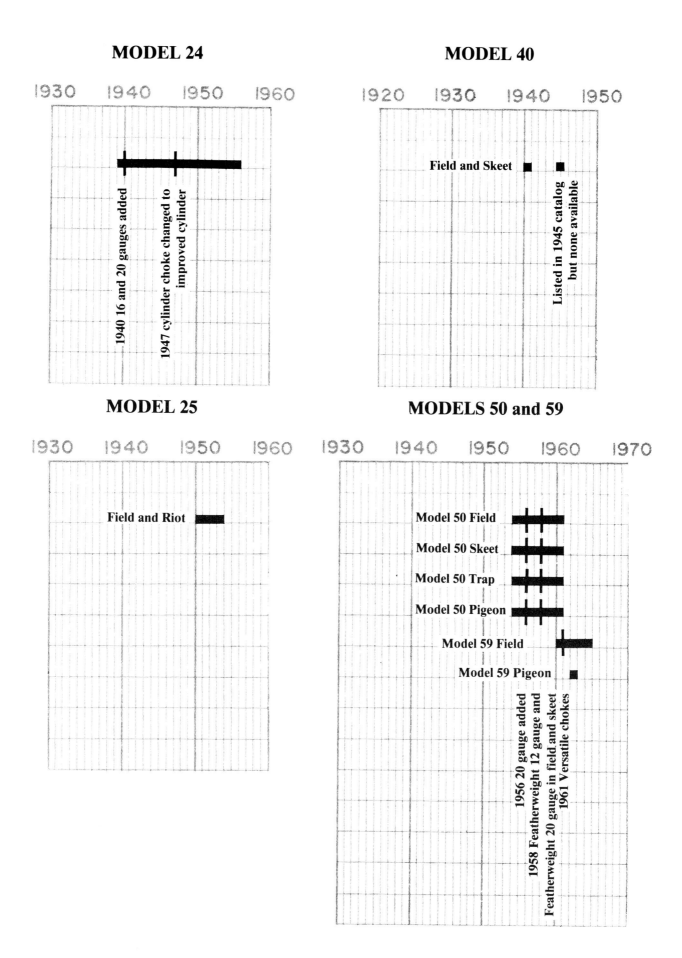

MODEL 24

1930 · 1940 · 1950 · 1960

1940 16 and 20 gauges added

1947 cylinder choke changed to improved cylinder

MODEL 40

1920 · 1930 · 1940 · 1950

Field and Skeet ■   ■ Listed in 1945 catalog but none available

MODEL 25

1930 · 1940 · 1950 · 1960

Field and Riot

MODELS 50 and 59

1930 · 1940 · 1950 · 1960 · 1970

Model 50 Field

Model 50 Skeet

Model 50 Trap

Model 50 Pigeon

Model 59 Field

Model 59 Pigeon

1956 20 gauge added

1958 Featherweight 12 gauge and Featherweight 20 gauge in field and skeet

1961 Versatile chokes

152

Another, bound in red leather. This one also had the tabs, and graph paper over each page for notes and changes.

A well used salesman's catalog specially bound in brown leather, with indexing tabs.

Appendix A

KNOWN PRINTED MATERIAL OTHER THAN BROCHURES WHICH DESCRIBE WINCHESTER ARMS MADE IN NEW HAVEN, CONNECTICUTT

WINCHESTER REPEATING ARMS CO. CATALOGS

Catalog Number	Date	Size	Remarks
	1867		1st known WRA Co. Catalog
	1869		
	1871		
	1873		
	1875		1st issue. Replica exists
	1875		2nd issue
	1876		
	3-1-1878	50 pp.*	Replica exists
	5-1-1878	5¾ × 8⁹⁄₁₆. 64 pp.	Replica exists
	8-1-1878	5¹¹⁄₁₆ × 8½. 63 pp.	
	5-1-1879		
	1880		
	8-1-1880		
	1-1-1881		
	3-1-1881		
	5-1-1881	5¹⁄₁₆ × 8⅝. 48 pp.	Features Hotchkiss
	4-1-1882		
	9-1-1882	64 pp.	Winchester & Hotchkiss
	6-1-1883	58 pp.	Winchester & Hotchkiss
	1-1-1884		
	9-1-1884	72 pp.	Winchester & Hotchkiss
	1-10-1885	72 pp.	Winchester & Hotchkiss
	11-1-1885	76 pp.	Winchester only
	1886		
	4-1886		
	10-1886	76 pp.	
	1-1887		
	6-1887	80 pp.	
	11-1887		
	5-1888	5⁹⁄₁₆ × 8⅝. 80 pp.	
	2-1889	5⅛ × 8⅝. 82 pp.	
	6-1889		
	2-1890	5¹¹⁄₁₆ × 8⅝. 82 pp.	
	6-1890		
	6-1890	5¹¹⁄₁₆ × 8⅝. 80 pp.	Seattle Branch
	7-1890	5¹¹⁄₁₆ × 8⅝. 80 pp.	
	11-1890	5¹¹⁄₁₆ × 8⁹⁄₁₆. 84 pp.	
	3-1891	5⁵⁄₁₆ × 8³⁄₁₆. 84 pp.	Replica exists
	8-1891	5⅝ × 8⅝. 84 pp.	
	1-1892	5¹¹⁄₁₆ × 8⅝. 84 pp.	
	7-1892	5⅝ × 8⅝. 84 pp.	
	10-1892	84 pp.	

154

A softbound catalog with cream cover and red and blue lettering, back cover featuring the then-new Model 12.

Form	Date	Size	Remarks
	12-1892	5⅝ × 8⅝. 84 pp.	
	2-1893	5¹¹⁄₁₆ × 8⁹⁄₁₆. 84 pp.	
	6-1893		
	10-1893	5⅝ × 8⅝. 94 pp.	
52	4-1894	5¹¹⁄₁₆ × 8⅝. 100 pp.	1st Known No. on Catalogs
53	11-1894	111 pp.	
54	2-1895	112 pp.	
55	8-1895	114 pp.	
56	1-1896	5⅝ × 8⁹⁄₁₆. 114 pp.	Replica exists
57	6-1896	5⅝ × 8¼. 128 pp.	
58	12-1896	5½ × 8½. 130 pp.	Replica exists
59	3-1897	5⅝ × 8⅜. 136 pp.	
60	11-1897	5½ × 8½. 148 pp.	
60	11-1897		(2nd Edition)
61	3-1898	5½ × 8½. 152 pp.	
62	10-1898	5⅝ × 8⅝. 158 pp.	
63	2-1899	5⅝ × 8⅝. 156 pp.	
64	8-1899	5¹³⁄₁₆ × 8½. 158 pp.	Salesmans Catalog. Leather bound tabs 7 round corners.*
65	2-1900		
65	4-1900	5⅜ × 8¼. 160 pp.	
66	10-1900	5⅝ × 8⅝. 164 pp.	
67	3-1901	5¼ × 8¼. 164 pp.	
68	1-1902	5⅝ × 8⅝. 164 pp.	
69	6-1902	5½ × 8¼. 164 pp.	
70	3-1903	5⅝ × 8⅝. 160 pp.	
	6-1904	5½ × 8¼. 164 pp.	
71	7-1904	5¹¹⁄₁₆ × 8½. 164 pp.	Salesman Catalog—Leather tabs & round corners
72	10-1905	5½ × 8³⁄₁₆. 170 pp.	Replica Exists
73	1-1907	5½ × 8¼. 176 pp.	Salesman Catlog—Leather tabs & round corners
74	3-1908	5½ × 8¼. 180 pp.	
75	3-1909	5⅛ × 8⅜. 182 pp.	Salesman Catalog—Leather tabs & round corners & graph paper over each page for notes and changes
76	6-1910	5½ × 8³⁄₁₆. 194 pp.	Salesman—same as #75
77	10-1911	5½ × 8⁷⁄₁₆. 202 pp.	
78	1-1913	5⅝ × 8⅝. 212 pp.	
78	1-1913		Larger—Heavier Paper
	1913		Entitled "Game Laws Blue Book Directory of Guides"
79	1-1914		Salesman Catalog—Leather
79	1914	5½ × 8⅜. 224 pp.	
80	1916	5½ × 8⅜. 224 pp.	Centennial Catalog with Oliver F. Winchester bust embossed on front
80	1916	5¹⁵⁄₁₆ × 8. 33 pp.	Supplement of 1-2-1917
80	1916		Supplement of 12-15-1917
81	1918	5½ × 8⅜. 213 pp.	Also Salesman Catalog—Bound tabs & round corners
81	9-15-1919		Revised
82	1920	7¾ × 10⅝. 208 pp.	
82	1920	8½ × 11. 208 pp.	Hard Bound
	3-15-1921		
	1923		
	1924		
83	1925	6 × 9. 88 pp.	

This Chinese red, cloth-bound specimen bears the company logo which became standard.

This salesman's catalog is bound in black leather and has the index tabs.

Form	Date	Size	Remarks
83	1925		Supplement of 3-1-1926
83	1925		Supplement of 8-1-1927
83	1925		Supplement of 1-3-1928
83	1925		Supplement of 7-1-1928
83	1925		Supplement of 1-2-1929
	1927		Small in size
	1927		Large in size
	1928		

Page numbers are the last numbered page. Oftentimes an index or blank pages appeared after the last numbered page.

In most instances regular, paper bound catalogs as well as Salesmans Catalogs were issued.

BLUE COVERED CATALOGS
WORLD STANDARD GUNS AND AMMUNITION

Catalog Number	Date	Size	Remarks
	7-1-1929	233 pp.	General Catalog
	None	5¾ × 7⅞. 233 pp.	General Catalog with 1930 rubber tired cannon
	None	116 pp.	Guns ammo only
	10-15-1930	5¾ × 7⅞. 233 pp.	General Catalog with dated gun list. Section view of Model 52 speed lock on page 156
	7-1931	5½ × 8. 116 pp.	Guns and ammo only undated with gun price list of Jan. 2, 1931. Insert shows new M/52 stock and trigger
	7-1931	5¼ × 7¾. 242 pp.	General Catalog
	7-1932	5⅜ × 7¾. 127 pp.	Guns and ammo only
	11-1932	5½ × 7⅝. 127 pp.	Guns and ammo only
	1933	5⅜ × 7¾. 144 pp.	Guns and ammo only with March 1, 1933 price list
89	1934	5½ × 7⅝. 152 pp.	Guns and ammo only last of numbered catalogs

158

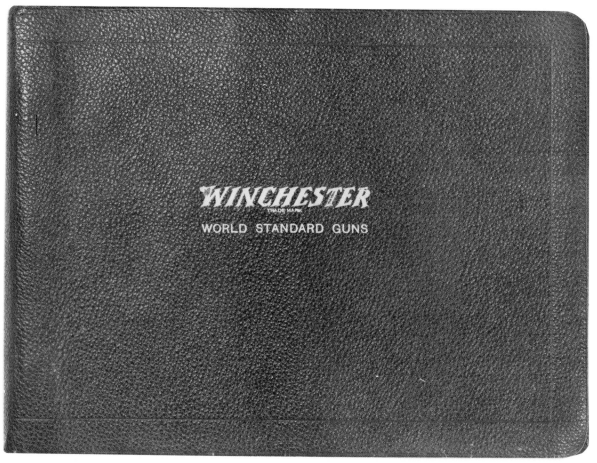

This sales promotion catalog contains 54 black and white glossy photographs, 8 × 10″, of the gun line, including engraving and carving available circa 1932. The gold logo and title are on black leather. Several of the photographs appear in this book.

This "scrapbook" catalog, ca 1930, is likely the rarest produced by Winchester. Its 273 pages, 8¾ × 11½″, cover the full line. The red WINCHESTER is embossed on the blue cloth binding.

WINCHESTER POCKET CATALOG OF GUNS AND AMMUNITION
MOST SAY "THE WINCHESTER STORE"

Catalog Number	Date	Size	Remarks
Form #250	12-1910	6⅛ × 3⅜. 28 pp.	Rifles & Shotguns
Form #C565	1921-22	3⅜ × 6¼. 28 pp.	Winchester Store
Form #634	1922		Fishing Tackle—Winchester Store
Form #673	1922	3⅛ × 6. 29 pp.	Winchester Store
Form #C722	1922	3⅛ × 6. 29 pp.	No Winchester Store
Form #C760	1923	3⅛ × 6. 29 pp.	Winchester Store
Form #761	1923	3⅛ × 6. 29 pp.	No Winchester Store
Form #759	1923	3⅛ × 6. 32 pp.	Winchester Store Tool Catalog
Form #910	1925(?)	6 × 3½. 32 pp.	General use—not store
Form #1266	?		Don't let your customers be disappointed (Not catalog)
Form #C910	1930(?)	3½ × 6. 32 pp.	Winchester Guns and Ammunition much like World Standard Catalogs

WORLD STANDARD GUNS AND AMMUNITION CATALOGS

Catalog Number	Date	Size	Remarks
Form #1262	1933	6⁵⁄₁₆ × 3⁵⁄₁₆. 60 pp.	
Form #1299	1934	6¼ × 3¼. 64 pp.	
Form #1368	1934	6⁵⁄₁₆ × 3¼. 64 pp.	
Form #1416	1936	6⁵⁄₁₆ × 3⁵⁄₁₆. 56 pp.	
Form #1460	1937	6⁵⁄₁₆ × 3⁵⁄₁₆. 56 pp.	
Form #1510	1938	6⁵⁄₁₆ × 3¹⁄₁₆. 56 pp.	
Form #1644	1939	6⅜ × 3³⁄₁₆. 56 pp.	
Form #1688	None	6⁵⁄₁₆ × 3⁵⁄₁₆. 56 pp.	
Form #1756	1940	6⅜ × 3⁵⁄₁₆. 52 pp.	2 variations (Back Cover)

RETAIL PRICE LIST OF WINCHESTER RIFLES AND SHOTGUNS

Form	Date	Size	Remarks
Form #905 4-26-10M	Mar 1, 1926	5½ × 8¾. 1 sheet	Issued with Catalog 83
Form #C-975- 3-28-10M	Jan 3, 1928	5½ × 8¾. 1 sheet	Issued with Catalog 83
Form #C-1041- 1-29-15M	Jan 2, 1929	5½ × 8½. 1 sheet	Issued with Catalog 83
Form #C-1041A 25M-1-31	Jan 2, 1931	7⅝ × 10⅜. 1 sheet	
Form #1265	Aug 12, 1933	4¾ × 7½. 4 pp.	
Form #1352	Sep 3, 1935	4⅝ × 8¼. 4 pp.	
Form #1442	Jan 2, 1937	4½ × 9½. 4 pp.	
Form #1530	Jan 22, 1938	5½ × 9½. 1 sheet, 6 frames	

This is the last of the numbered catalogs. The cover is blue with red company logo.

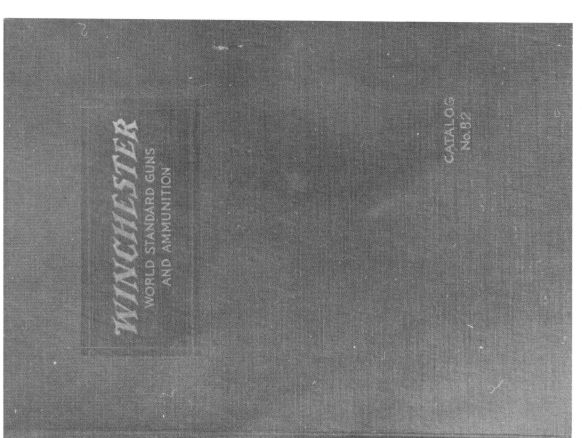

Salesman's edition with tabs, 8 × 10¾".

RETAIL PRICE LIST WINCHESTER RIFLES AND SHOTGUNS

Form	Date	Size	Remarks
Form #1239	Mar 1, 1933	8⅜ × 11. 15 pp.	
Form #1219	Feb 24, 1934	8¹⁄₁₆ × 11. 18 pp.	
Form #1522	Jan 22, 1938	8¾ × 10⅞. 29 pp.	
Form #1694	Jul 1, 1940	5¾ × 3¼. 19 pp.	
Form #1788	Nov 13, 1941	5¾ × 3¼. 13 pp.	
Form #1825	Jan 22, 1945	5⅞ × 3¼. 13 pp.	
Form #1860	Oct 1, 1946	8½ × 10¾. 46 pp.	
Form #1864R	Mar 24, 1947	5⅞ × 3³⁄₁₆. 13 pp.	
Form #1860R	May 1, 1947	8¾ × 10¾. 46 pp.	
Form #1980	Jan 14, 1949	5⅞ × 3¼. 14 pp.	
Form #1972	Jan 14, 1949	8¼ × 10¾. 49 pp.	
Form #2061	Dec 15, 1950	5½ × 3³⁄₁₆. 12 pp.	
Form #2050	Dec 15, 1950	8½ × 10⅝. 59 pp.	Retail Price List and General Catalog of Arms and Accessories
Form #2082 3-52	Jan 2, 1952	4¾ × 7⅛. 29 pp.	
Form #2152	Jan 2, 1954	4½ × 7. 29 pp.	
Form #2137	Jan 2, 1954	4⅝ × 7⅛. 33 pp.	
Form #2137	Jan 24, 1955	4⅝ × 7⅛. 33 pp.	
Form #2137 REV	Dec 30, 1955	4⅝ × 7. 36 pp.	
Form #2272	Dec 15, 1956	4½ × 7. 36 pp.	
	Jan 2, 1958	4½ × 6⅞. 41 pp.	

CATALOG OR RETAIL PRICE LIST OF WINCHESTER ARMS AND ACCESSORIES

Form	Date	Size	Remarks
Form #1753R	Jun 10, 1941	7¾ × 10¾. 45 pp.	
Form #1835R	?	5½ × 7½. 46 pp.	
Form #1937	1948	5⅜ × 7⅜. 44 pp.	
Form #1972	Jan 14, 1949	8⅜ × 10¾. 49 pp.	
Form #2012	?	5½ × 7½. 54 pp.	General Catalog

WHOLESALE-RETAIL PRICE LIST
WINCHESTER ARMS AND ACCESSORIES OR WINCHESTER RIFLES AND SHOTGUNS

Form	Date	Size	Remarks
Form #C-622	Jan 3, 1922	7½ × 10⅜. 8 pp.	
Form #C-763	Jan 2, 1923	7½ × 10⅜. 8 pp.	
Form #1220	Jun 21, 1932	6¾ × 10½. 12 pp.	No illustrations
Form #1282	Feb 24, 1934	8¼ × 10⅞. 18 pp.	
Form #1395	Feb 2, 1936	8 × 10⅜. 19 pp.	
Form #1439	Jan 2, 1937	9¼ × 10⅞. 27 pp.	
Form #1521	Jan 22, 1938	9⅜ × 11. 38 pp.	
Form #1604-WR	Mar 4, 1939	9¼ × 11. 35 pp.	
Form #1652	Jan 2, 1940	9⅜ × 11. 47 pp.	
Form #1691-W-R	Jul 1, 1940	9¼ × 11. 47 pp.	
Form #1817	Jan 22, 1945	8½ × 11. 43 pp.	
Form #1833WR	Mar 7, 1946	7¾ × 10¾. 45 pp.	
Form #1858	Oct 1, 1946	8⅜ × 10¾. 46 pp.	
Form #1971	Jan 14, 1949	8½ × 10¾. 49 pp.	
Form #2048	Dec 15, 1950	8⅜ × 10¾. 58 pp.	Also General Catalog
Form #2160	Jan 2, 1953	8½ × 11. 16 pp.	This and subsequent lists titled Winchester Rifles & Shotguns Wholesale-Retail Price List
Form #2114	Jan 2, 1953	8½ × 11. 16 pp.	
Form #2132	Jan 2, 1954	8½ × 11. 16 pp.	
Form #2185	Jan 24, 1955	8½ × 11. 20 pp.	
Form #2225	Dec 30, 1955	8½ × 11. 30 pp.	
Form #2271	Dec 15, 1956	8½ × 11. 30 pp.	
Form #2292	Jan 2, 1958	8½ × 11. 30 pp.	
Form #2309	Jan 2, 1959	8½ × 11. 25 pp.	
Form #2346	Jan 2, 1960	8½ × 11. 18 pp.	
Form #1F001A	Jan 2, 1961	8½ × 11. 18 pp.	
Form #2F001A	Jan 2, 1962	8½ × 11. 18 pp.	
Form #3F001A	Jan 2, 1963	8½ × 10⅞. 20 pp.	
4FWRPL (200M)	Jan 2, 1964	8½ × 11. 19 pp.	
WM 101 REV 2	Jan 2, 1965	8½ × 11. 39 pp.	
WM 167	Jan 3, 1966	8½ × 11. 16 pp.	
WM 224	Jan 3, 1967	8⅜ × 10⅞. 20 pp.	
Form #3001	Jan 2, 1973	8½ × 11. 20 pp.	Winchester Firearms Price List Wholesale/Retail
Form #6011	Jan 2, 1976	8½ × 11. 12 pp.	Winchester Firearms Price List Wholesale/Retail

DISTRIBUTOR PRICE LISTS

Form	Date	Size	Remarks
Form #1970	Jan 14, 1949	$8\frac{3}{8} \times 10\frac{7}{8}$. 50 pp.	Winchester Arms and Accessories
Form #2012	Feb 2, 1950	$8\frac{3}{8} \times 10\frac{7}{8}$. 56 pp.	Distributor Price List and General Catalog Winchester Arms and Accessories
Form #2012	Sep 12, 1950	$8\frac{3}{8} \times 10\frac{7}{8}$. 56 pp.	Distributor Price List and General Catalog Winchester Arms and Accessories
Form #2049	Dec 15, 1950	$8\frac{3}{8} \times 10\frac{7}{8}$. 60 pp.	Distributor Price List and General Catalog Winchester Arms and Accessories
Form #2058	Jan 8, 1951	$8\frac{3}{8} \times 10\frac{5}{8}$. 20 pp.	Winchester Arms and Accessories
Form #2074	Jan 2, 1952	$8\frac{1}{2} \times 10\frac{7}{8}$. 20 pp.	Winchester Arms and Accessories
Form #2113	Jan 2, 1953	$8\frac{1}{2} \times 11$. 18 pp.	Winchester Rifles and Shotguns
Form #2130	Jan 2, 1954	$8\frac{1}{2} \times 11$. 18 pp.	Winchester Rifles and Shotguns
Form #2186	Jan 24, 1955	$8\frac{1}{2} \times 11$. 22 pp.	Winchester Rifles and Shotguns
Form #2224	Dec 30, 1955	$8\frac{1}{2} \times 11$. 32 pp.	Winchester Rifles and Shotguns
Form #2276	Dec 15, 1956	$8\frac{1}{2} \times 11$. 32 pp.	Winchester Firearms 1957
Form #2290	Jan 2, 1959	$8\frac{1}{2} \times 11$. 32 pp.	Winchester Rifles and Shotguns
Form #2345	Jan 2, 1960	$8\frac{1}{2} \times 11$. 20 pp.	Winchester Rifles and Shotguns
1F001B	Jan 3, 1961	$8\frac{1}{2} \times 11$. 20 pp.	Winchester Rifles and Shotguns
2F0016	Jan 2, 1962	$8\frac{1}{2} \times 11$. 20 pp.	Winchester Rifles and Shotguns
3F001B	Jan 2, 1963	$8\frac{1}{2} \times 11$. 22 pp.	Winchester Rifles and Shotguns
4FDPL(5m)	Jan 2, 1964	$8\frac{1}{2} \times 11$. 20 pp.	Same with March 25 Price Changes
WM 100	Jan 2, 1965	$8\frac{1}{2} \times 11$. 40 pp.	Winchester Rifles and Shotguns
WM 166	Jan 3, 1966	$8\frac{1}{2} \times 11$. 16 pp.	Winchester Firearms Price List
WM 225	Jan 3, 1967	$8\frac{1}{2} \times 11$. 20 pp.	Winchester Firearms Price List
WM 282	Jan 2, 1968	$8\frac{3}{8} \times 10\frac{7}{8}$. 20 pp.	Winchester Firearms Price List
Form #2002D	Jan 3, 1972	$8\frac{3}{8} \times 10\frac{7}{8}$. 20 pp.	Winchester Firearms Price List

WINCHESTER AND WESTERN SPORTING ARMS AND AMMUNITION

Form	Date	Size	Remarks
Form #2359 REV	1960	$8\frac{1}{2} \times 11$. 36 pp.	
Form #1AF001	1961	$8\frac{1}{2} \times 11$. 36 pp.	
Form #2AF001	1962	10×7. 31 pp.	
Form #3AF002	1963	$10\frac{3}{4} \times 8\frac{1}{2}$. 31 pp.	
Form #4AF001	1964	$8\frac{1}{2} \times 10\frac{7}{8}$. 35 pp.	
Form #WM107	1965	$8\frac{3}{8} \times 10\frac{7}{8}$. 39 pp.	
Form #WM153	1966	$8\frac{1}{2} \times 10\frac{3}{4}$. 31 pp.	Norman Rockwell Stagecoach scene on cover
Form #WM208	1967	$8\frac{1}{2} \times 10\frac{7}{8}$. 39 pp.	
Form #WM274	1968	$8\frac{1}{4} \times 11$. 47 pp.	
Form #WM495	1969	$8\frac{1}{4} \times 11$. 47 pp.	
Form #WM90	1970	$8\frac{1}{4} \times 11$. 47 pp.	
Form #0-97	1971	$8\frac{1}{4} \times 10\frac{7}{8}$. 47 pp.	Special NRA Centennial Edition
Form #2001	1972	$8\frac{1}{4} \times 10\frac{3}{4}$. 47 pp.	
Form #3030	1973	$8\frac{3}{16} \times 10\frac{11}{16}$. 47 pp.	
Form #4001	1974	$8\frac{1}{4} \times 10\frac{3}{4}$. 31 pp.	
Form #5001	1975	$8\frac{1}{4} \times 10\frac{3}{4}$. 31 pp.	
Form #6001	1976	$8\frac{1}{2} \times 11$. 39 pp.	Bicentennial Edition
Form #7001	1977	$8\frac{1}{2} \times 11$. 39 pp.	
Form #7001	1977	$5\frac{5}{8} \times 7\frac{1}{2}$. 39 pp.	
Form #P101	1978	$5\frac{1}{2} \times 7\frac{1}{2}$. 47 pp.	
Form #P160-11/78	1979	$5\frac{1}{2} \times 7\frac{1}{2}$. 39 pp.	
Form #323 80	1980	$8\frac{1}{2} \times 11$. 40 pp.	
Form #323	1980	$5\frac{5}{8} \times 7\frac{5}{16}$.	
Form #323-81	1981	$8\frac{3}{8} \times 10\frac{3}{4}$. 39 pp.	

MISCELLANEOUS CATALOGS

Form	Date	Size	Remarks
	1895 or later	9 × 6. 15 pp.	Winchester Lee Straight Pull Rifle Caliber .236
	10-1897	9 × 6. 28 pp.	Highly Finished Arms Reprint Exists
Form #1264	1933	9 × 6. 24 pp.	Winchester Model 21 Double
Form #1423	1938?	9 × 6. 24 pp.	Winchester Model 21 America's Finest Development in Double Guns
Form #2037	1952–53?	8½ × 11. 68 pp.	Winchester Firearms
Form #2111	1953	6 × 9. 28 pp.	Winchester Model 21 Double
	1955	8½× 11. 79 pp.	Winchester Firearms 1855–1955 Shows all current models
Form #2247-IMP-IMM-456		7 × 10. 24 pp.	The Story of Winchester The Gun That Won The West. This is the "comic book" promotion piece
4PG(50M)	1964	8½ × 11. 32 pp.	A Guide to Successful Shooting The 1964 line of Winchester-Western Products . . . Proven on Safari
		8½ × 11.	The Winchester Model 21 (Theme binder with 21 catalog, 21 and 12 order blanks and engraving)
		11 × 8½. 10 pp.	Winchester Model 21
WM-279	1967	8½ × 8½. 26 pp.	Winchester World-Wide Safaris
Form #3077 REV 5/74	1976	8½ × 11. 8 pp.	Winchester-Western Firearms and Ammunition for the Modern Law Enforcement Officer
	1980	8¼ × 11. 5 pp.	Perazzi Trap, Skeet, Live Bird and Field Gun
Form #WM29	1980?	9½ × 6½. 10 pp. with cover	Winchester Firearms. Winchester and Western Ammunition First in the Line of Duty (Law Enforcement catalog)
Form #601-10-80	1980	8½ ×11. 14 pp.	Winchester High Performance Products for Law Enforcement
	1982–83	11½ × 9⅛. 8 pp.	Winchester Model 21 (plus letters re 28/410 and 20/28/410)

SALES PROMOTION MATERIALS

Form	Date	Size	Remarks
	1931–1933	8½ × 11 plus binder, 270 pp.	Winchester Sales Manual with tabs and price lists. World Standard Guns and Ammunition, Flashlights and Batteries, etc.
	1932	12 × 9. 54 pp.	Black Leather 3-Ring Binder, Winchester Trade Mark World Standard Guns, 54 black and white glossies, including current models and engraving and carving for rifles and shotguns, and case for high grade cutlery
	1938	8¼ × 10¾. 66 pp.	Winchester Sales Manual (Also reprint)
Form #2002	1-1949	8½ × 11. 79 pp.	Winchester Gun Salesman's Handbook second edition. Slick cover
	1954?	9 × 12. 15 pp.	Western and Winchester The Most Famous Names in Sporting Arms and Ammunition has Model 50 brochure stapled in center fold
	1955	8½ × 11. 77 pp.	Winchester Gun Salesman's Handbook (Slick cover)
WR6-575011	1957	8½ × 11. 77pp.	Firearms (yellow cover)
	1960?	27 heavy sheets in red plaid 3-ring binder	Winchester-Western Product Sales Guide
Form #FO14	1962	9 × 11. Pages not numbered (40 pp. total)	Winchester-Western Product Sales Guide
Form #2F014	1962	9 × 11. Pages not numbered (40 pp. total)	Winchester-Western Product Sales Guide
	1963?	14 × 11. 16 pp.	A Dynamic Approach to Firearms Selling
	1963	11 × 8½. 24 pp.	Product Sales Guide
	1966	8⅝ × 11⅜.	Winchester Franchise Gun Club Program
	10-27-1966	9 × 12.	Centennial Press Kit
Form #WM270	1967	8½ × 11. 66 pp.	Hunting for Profits by Paul M. Doane
	1969	9 × 12.	Astronauts Receive "Golden Spike Carbines
	1972	8½ × 11.	Important 1972 Price Information for Dealers (perfect binder for all 72 catalogs and lists)
	1975		Many heavy sheets and Sporting Arms, Ammunition and Reloading Components, Winchester Firearms Price List, and Winchester and Western Sporting Ammunition Price List in red 3-ring binder
	1976	8½ × 11. 8 pp.	Winchester Western 1976 In-Store Dealer Programs
	1977	9 × 12.	Press Kit. Limited Edition 94
	1977	8½ × 11.	Going Great Guns Sales Award Campaign
	1978?	8½ × 11. Many pages of clip outs for advertising copy	Winchester Western Advertising Kit
	1979	9 × 11¾	Press Kit Models 94 and 9422
	1979	9 × 11¾	Press Kit Limited Edition 94

COMPONENT PARTS

Form	Date	Size	Remarks
Form #C-584	Nov 15, 1921	7½ × 10⅝. 16 pp.	Catalog of Component Parts for Winchester Rifles & Shotguns. . . .
Form #C-943	Mar 15, 1927	8¼ × 11. 28 pp.	Catalog of Component Parts for Winchester Rifles & Shotguns. . . .
Form #1018B	Jan 15, 1929	8 × 11. 36 pp.	Catalog of Component Parts for Winchester Rifles & Shotguns, Rifle & Shotgun Sights
Form #1018B	Apr 15, 1931	7½ × 10¾. 39 pp.	Catalog of Component Parts for Winchester Rifles & Shotguns, Rifle & Shotgun Sights
Form #1297	May 1, 1934	7¾ × 10¾. 53 pp.	Catalog of Component Parts for Winchester Rifles & Shotguns. . . .
Form #1624	Jun 1, 1939	8⅜ × 10⅞. 71 pp.	Catalog of Component Parts for Winchester Rifles & Shotguns, Rifle & Shotgun Sights
Form #1802	Jul 1, 1942	8⅛ × 10¾. 74 pp.	Catalog of Component Parts for Winchester Rifles & Shotguns. . . .
Form #1802	Mar 7, 1946 Sticker so dated	8¼ × 10¾. 74 pp. Raise prices by 15%	Catalog of Component Parts for Winchester Rifles & Shotguns, Rifle & Shotgun Sights
Form #1802	Oct 1, 1946 Sticker so dated	8⅜ × 10¾. 74 pp. Raise prices by 27%	Catalog of Component Parts for Winchester Rifles & Shotguns, Rifle & Shotgun Sights
Form #1899	Jan 16, 1948	8½ × 11. 85 pp.	Catalog of Component Parts for Winchester Rifles & Shotguns, Rifle & Shotgun Sights, Accessories
Form #1899	Jan 14, 1949 Sticker so dated	8⅛ × 11. 85 pp. Raise prices by 5%	Catalog of Component Parts for Winchester Rifles & Shotguns, Rifle & Shotgun Sights, Accessories
Form #2004	Jan 14, 1949	8½ × 11. 92 pp.	Catalog of Component Parts for Winchester Rifles & Shotguns, Rifle & Shotgun Sights, Accessories
	Dec 15, 1950	82 × 11. 116 pp.	Catalog of Component Parts for Winchester Rifles & Shotguns, Rifle & Shotgun Sights, Accessories—slick cover
Form #2165	Jul 1, 1954	8⅜ × 11. 92 pp.	Component Parts, Sights, Accessories—slick cover
	Jul 1, 1956	11 × 8½. 99 pp.	Component Parts, Sights, Accessories for Firearms—slick cover
	Jun 1, 1960	11 × 8½. 103 pp.	Component Parts, Sights, Accessories for Firearms—slick cover
	Jan 2, 1962	8½ × 11. 75 pp.	Winchester Firearms Component Parts
	1967	8½ × 11. 64 pp.	Winchester Firearms Component Parts
	1969	8½ × 11. 64 pp.	Winchester Firearms Component Parts
	1975	8½ × 11. 68 pp.	Winchester Firearms Component Parts Catalog
	1978	8½ × 11. 68 pp.	Winchester Firearms Component Parts Catalog
	1979	8½ × 11. 76 pp.	Winchester Firearms Component Parts Catalog
	1980	8½ × 11. 72 pp.	Winchester Firearms Component Parts Catalog
	1981	8½ × 11. 74 pp.	Winchester Firearms Component Parts Catalog

Appendix B

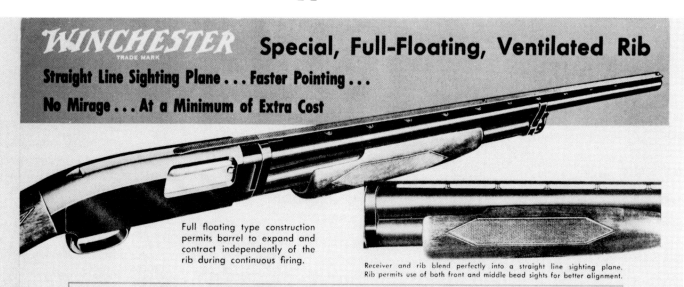

WINCHESTER
Special, Full-Floating, Ventilated Rib

**Straight Line Sighting Plane ... Faster Pointing ...
No Mirage ... At a Minimum of Extra Cost**

Full floating type construction permits barrel to expand and contract independently of the rib during continuous firing.

Receiver and rib blend perfectly into a straight line sighting plane. Rib permits use of both front and middle bead sights for better alignment.

WINCHESTER MODEL 12 AND MODEL 42 SHOTGUNS WITH WINCHESTER SPECIAL VENTILATED RIB

MODEL 12 MAGNUM DUCK GUN

Symbol	Gauge	Barrel	Suggested *Retail Each	Suggested *Wholesale Each
G1262SV	12	30" Full Choke	$143.70	$107.80

MODEL 12 SKEET GUN

Symbol	Gauge	Barrel	Suggested *Retail Each	Suggested *Wholesale Each
G1213SV	12	26" Winchester Skeet Choke	$161.90	$121.50
G1215SV	20			
G1217SV	28			

MODEL 12 SKEET GUN WITH CUTTS COMPENSATOR

Symbol	Gauge	Barrel	Suggested *Retail Each	Suggested *Wholesale Each
G1212SV	12	Cutts Compensator Steel, 26"	$176.15	$132.15
G1214SV	20			
G1216SV	28			
The above guns fitted with stock and extension slide handle of selected walnut, if available			$188.90	$141.65

MODEL 12 TRAP GUN

Symbol	Gauge	Barrel	Retail	Wholesale
G1258SV	12	30" Full Choke	$166.40	$124.85

MODEL 12 TRAP GUN (Monte Carlo Stock)

Symbol	Gauge	Barrel	Retail	Wholesale
G1209SV	12	30" Full Choke	$174.70	$131.15

MODEL 12 PIGEON GRADE

	Retail	Wholesale
Field Gun, Winchester Special Ventilated Rib	$210.05	$168.05
Skeet Gun, Winchester Special Ventilated Rib	$210.05	$168.05
Trap Gun, Winchester Special Ventilated Rib	$215.60	$172.50
Magnum Duck Gun, Winchester Special Ventilated Rib	$221.10	$176.90

MODEL 42 SKEET GUN

Symbol	Chamber	Barrel	Suggested *Retail Each	Suggested *Wholesale Each
G4287SV	2½" Shells – only	28" Winchester Skeet Choke	$127.45	$ 95.30
G4285SV	3" Shells			
The above guns fitted with stock and extension slide handle of selected American walnut, if available......			$139.70	$104.80
G4288SV	2½" Shells – only	Cutts Compensator Steel, 28"	$154.05	$115.45
G4286SV	3" Shells			
The above guns fitted with stock and extension slide handle of selected American walnut, if available......			$166.65	$124.95

MODEL 42 DELUXE

	Retail	Wholesale
Model 42 DeLuxe, Winchester Special Ventilated Rib....	$192.90	$154.30

* U.S. Excise Tax Included

The above Wholesale and Retail prices are the minimum prices established by us in all states that have Fair Trade Laws. All Prices are subject to change without notice.

Winchester Special Ventilated Ribs are sold only on new guns and factory installed. In addition to the above listed Winchester Model 12's and Model 42's, Winchester Special Ventilated Rib will be furnished on special order, at extra charge, on all Model 12 and Model 42 Field Guns and on interchangeable barrels for Model 12's and Model 42's equipped with Winchester Special Ventilated Rib. See Price List dated January 2, 1954 for complete schedule of charges.

Olin
ARMS and AMMUNITION DIVISION • OLIN INDUSTRIES, INC.
NEW HAVEN 4 • CONNECTICUT

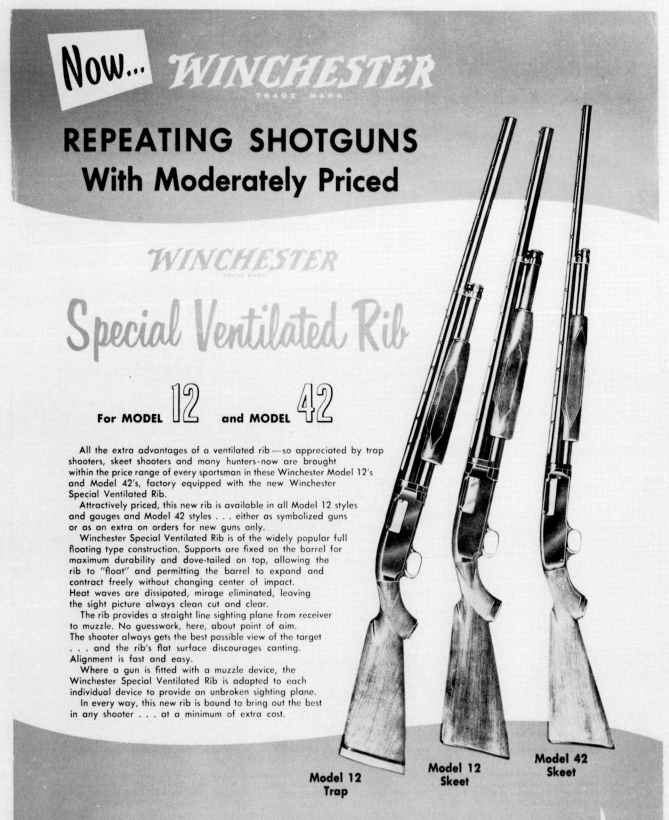

Appendix C
SERIAL NUMBERS

In most instances, owners of Winchester shotguns must be content to estimate when they were manufactured, shipped from the factory, or sold. What is known about serial numbers from 1866 through approximately 1907 resides in the Winchester Museum. Persons interested in dating a gun should send the model and serial number and $15.00 to Winchester Museum, Box 1000, Cody, WY 82414. If Museum personnel cannot date a gun the fee will be refunded.

Information about serial numbers between 1907 and 1962 has to be generated from purchase records or first owner recollection—treacherous at best. U.S. Repeating Arms Company has records since 1962 and will respond to inquiries. The late model 12's and 21's may be dated this way. Especially in the case of 21's, it is pointless to interpolate from a table of serial numbers because receivers were made up years before they were used as orders came in.

Dates for most serial numbers are not available because records were not always kept and because records were lost to fire, remodeling, and the like. These should be distrusted because they could only be constructed accurately by examining a great many guns and establishing when they were purchased—which only approximates when they were manufactured.

Because of production flow, it is not altogether well to specify that a serial number started a production year. During much of the time that the models described in this book were in production, Winchester hired outside contractors to manufacture receivers in the plant. Receivers were stamped serially as they were made up, oiled, and placed in boxes for storage. Later assemblers took boxes out of storage and put receivers in bins at their workplaces. Because receivers were not stored or selected by number by the several assemblers, the result was chaos. Museum personnel have found many numbers as far as three to five years out of order.

Almost from the beginning Mr. A. E. Hertel was in charge of the numbering department. In 1934, approximately 30 of his small notebooks were put in the Winchester vault. A few were added later. The Museum acquired these in 1982. Mr. William L. Porter, research associate, used them to prepare data for the following pages. ·

MODEL 1887

SN 1	Apr 15, 1887
SN 6950	Jan 4, 1888
SN 21205	Jan 8, 1890
SN 21000-21130	all in 1888

A few 1889 in SN range 21152 to 21200 then almost all 1890.
A large number of guns made in 1889 found in SN range 22,150 to 25,300.

SN 35301	Jan 3, 1890
About SN 28668	Jan 6, 7, 1891
About SN 38761	Jan 5, 1892
About SN 49062	Jan 9, 1893
About SN 54350	Jan 9, 1894
About SN 56250	Jan 2, 1895
About SN 58967	Jan 9, 1896
About SN 59911	Jan 5, 1897
About SN 62050	Jan 3, 1898

A few (very few) Model 87's made in early 1899
Model 1901's begin with SN 64856 Sep 17–26, 1901

MODEL 1901/01

SN 64856	Sep 17–26, 1901
SN 67000	Around Jun, 1902
SN 67800	Around Jun, 1903
SN 67800	Around Jun 7, 1905

Note: So few made in 1904 that a span is impossible.
About 72,100 guns made in 1906 began to appear.
About 72,600 guns made in 1907 began to appear.

At 72700	Mar, Jun and Jul, 1909

Only a few made in 1908

MODEL 1893

SN 1 made Dec 30, 1893
SN 2 made May 26, 1893
SN 3 made May 6, 1894
SN 4 made Jun 29, 1893
SN 5 made Jan 27, 1893
SN 6103 made Jan 6, 1894
SN 6113 made Jan 6, 1894
Starting about SN 7000 majority on paper made in 1894
Starting at SN 16400 majority on paper made in 1895
Starting about SN 23900 majority on paper made in 1896
Starting about SN 31971 majority on paper made in 1897
    34050 = end of 1893's

MODEL 1897/97

34,241-63,633 numbered June 2, 1897–Dec. 28, 1898
63,634-89,665 numbered Dec. 29, 1898–Dec. 13, 1899
89,666-133,322 numbered Dec. 17, 1899–Apr. 16, 1901
133,323-154,666 numbered Apr. 16, 1901–Dec. 20, 1901
154,667-191,344 numbered Dec. 20, 1901–Dec. 13, 1902
191,345-230,004 numbered Dec. 13, 1902–Dec. 16, 1903
230,005-268,760 numbered Dec. 17, 1903–Dec. 21, 1904
268,761-308,192 numbered Dec. 22, 1904–Dec. 15, 1905
308,193-352,131 numbered Dec. 16, 1905–Dec. 22, 1906
352,132-387,844 numbered Dec. 22, 1906–Dec. 4, 1907
387,845-420,996 numbered Dec. 4, 1907–Dec. 22, 1908
420,997-457,282 numbered Dec. 22, 1908–June 14, 1909
457,283-488,825 numbered June 15, 1909–June 3, 1910
488,826-520,546 numbered June 4, 1910–Mar. 22, 1911
520,547-568,874 numbered Mar. 24, 1911–Oct. 2, 1912
568,875-583,887 numbered Oct. 3, 1912–Apr. 11, 1913
583,888-600,726 numbered Apr. 12, 1913–Oct. 4, 1914
600,727-622,264 numbered Oct. 6, 1914–Feb. 3, 1915
622,265-644,513 numbered Feb. 4, 1915–Sept. 14, 1916
644,514-684,886 numbered Sept. 16, 1916–Apr. 30, 1918

Now a Skip

734,634-741,527 numbered Sept. 11, 1920–Oct. 29, 1920
741,528-753,642 numbered Oct. 29, 1920–May 11, 1922
753,643-766,451 numbered May 12, 1922–Apr. 6, 1923
766,452-799,478 numbered Apr. 7, 1923–Dec. 16, 1923
779,479-803,251 numbered Dec. 17, 1923–Aug. 28, 1925
803,252-808,658 numbered Aug. 29, 1925–Mar. 19, 1926
808,659-826,658 numbered Mar. 23, 1926–Oct. 27, 1927
826,659-829,830 numbered Oct. 29, 1926–Jan. 10, 1928
829,831-831,618 numbered Jan. 11, 1928–Feb. 17, 1928
831,619-833,224 numbered Feb. 20, 1928–Mar. 23, 1928
833,225-835,621 numbered Mar. 28, 1928–May 17, 1928
835,622-844,620 numbered May 21, 1928–Dec. 13, 1928
844,620-852,643 numbered Dec. 14, 1928–June 29, 1929
852,644-856,628 numbered July 3, 1929–Dec. 2, 1929
856,629-862,797 numbered Dec. 3, 1929–June 27, 1930
862,798-871,836 numbered July 10, 1930–Nov. 5, 1931
871,837-877,076 numbered Nov. 9, 1931–Jan. 25, 1932
877,077-916,216 numbered Jan. 26, 1931–Oct. 16, 1940

Appendix D
WHAT OUR CUSTOMERS WANT AND EXPECT IN A WINCHESTER (extracted from an internal document of the Winchester Repeating Arms Co.)

MODEL 12
REPEATING SHOTGUN
ALL STYLES

WHAT OUR CUSTOMERS EXPECT

RECEIVER and ACTION — Well polished—Dulite finish; non-glare sand blast finish on top of receiver for Trap and Skeet guns.

Receiver rib on Trap and Skeet styles, centered on receiver top—lined up and in same place as barrel rib.

Face of breech bolt smooth, free from burrs, all cams burnished and polished.

Guard fitting close and polished to conform with contour and fit of receiver to give good match.

Trigger lock functioning smoothly—no binding.

Trigger adjusted to clean, let-off 4-½–6 lbs.

Action slide lock release easily operative.

Action to work smoothly without roughness or binding—positive feeding, extraction and ejection.

Actions correctly timed, triple safety features fully operative.

BARREL and MAGAZINE — Dulite blue finish over well polished exterior—no circular thread-like marks.

Interior surfaces highly polished, free from any impressions or tool marks.

Chamber perfectly round, concentric, no tool tears or marks—not oversize.

Front sight properly centered and seated without protruding into barrel.

Ventilated ribs securely attached, correctly positioned at proper height directly over center of bore; lining up with and in same plane with receiver rib.

Magazine—Dulite—sand blast finish. No binding of shells, fitted with transformer limiting capacity to two shells. Turns easily when unlocking to take down the gun.

STOCK and SLIDE HANDLE — Of dense grain walnut, lacquer finish free from flaking, runs, or bubbles. Stock abutting the receiver uniformly around its circumference with very little excess wood.

Butt plate neatly fitted.

Recoil pad (on trap styles) neatly fitted.

Slide handle centered to avoid rubbing barrel.

Checkering (trap and skeet styles and Pigeon Grade) to be clean, sharp, no run over into border. Border of checkering clean, no tearing, gouging or undulations.

Dimensions of stocks to be within ⅛″ of those published in catalog—1/16″ for Trap guns.

PATTERNS — Percentage of shot load in 30″ circle at 40 yards.

Full choke—	approximately 70%
Imp. Mod. choke—	approximately 65%
Modified choke—	approximately 50%
Imp. Cylinder—	approximately 40%

Charge to be centered within 1″ any direction from aiming point at 40 yards.

GENERAL — Easy to put together and take down without undue force or difficulty.

Action free from metal filings, chips, or any foreign matter except light grease for protection.

Careful wrapping and packing to prevent blemishing or damage in shipment.

TRAP AND SKEET GUNS

STOCK and EXTENSION SLIDE HANDLE — Selected American Walnut—steel cap on pistol grip, recoil pad on Trap guns—both nicely fitted.

PIGEON GRADE

STOCK and EXTENSION — Full fancy American Walnut, smoothly and carefully finished—no sanding marks. Pistol grip cap, buttplate or recoil pad all nicely fitted. Fancy checkering of best quality, clean, sharp and neatly done. Stock and handle well matched in grain and color. Stock and receiver to be perfectly matched where they join at grip.

ACTION — Hand smoothed working parts.
Breech bolt and carrier engine turned.
Action to be adjusted for smooth easy operation.

BARREL — Extra polish for finest finish.
Pigeon engraved on barrel extension.

174

MODEL 37

SINGLE SHOT SHOTGUN

WHAT OUR CUSTOMERS EXPECT—

FRAME
and
ACTION
— Dulite blue finish on polished exterior.
Top lever to center when gun is closed.
Frame and barrel to fit well and lock properly.
Gun to close easily—no binding—properly honed extractor.
Cocking lever to operate and release smoothly.
Firing pin to strike correctly—no off center blows.
Positive ejection.
Shells to load in chamber properly—no bypassing extractor.

BARREL
— Dulite blue finish on polished exterior.
Interior surfaces well polished—no tool marks.
Front sight correctly located, seated and no protrusion into barrel.
Barrel lug correctly centered and solidly brazed.

STOCK
and
FOREARM
— Correctly shaped of American walnut. Stock neatly abutted to frame—no excessive overlapping of wood to metal. Neatly fitted butt plate. Forearm properly fitted to barrel lug—minimum effort to remove or replace.
Lacquer finish lustrous, free from flaking, runs or bubbles.

PATTERNS
— With commercial loads. 30" circle at 40 yards.

Choked— approximately 67%
Modified— approximately 50%

Center of pattern within 2" of aiming point in any direction.

GENERAL
— Action free of metal filings, chips or other foreign matter except light grease for protection.
Adequate wrapping and packing to prevent blemishing or damage in shipment.

MODEL 42
SLIDE ACTION .410 GA. SHOTGUN

WHAT OUR CUSTOMERS EXPECT—

RECEIVER
and
ACTION
— Dulite finish on well polished exterior.
Side plate carefully fitted—screws flush.
Guard well matched to receiver.
Action operating smoothly—without roughness or binding.
Positive feeding, extraction, and ejection—no dropping of shells.
Action timed carefully to prevent discharge unless action is fully locked.
Trigger lock positive—no binding.
Action slide release easily operative.
Handle 2-½ and 3" shells equally well.
Trigger adjusted to clean, crisp let-off at 4-½ lbs.
Matting on receiver top correctly aligned.

BARREL — Dulite finish over well polished exterior—free from circular thread-
and   like appearance.
MAGAZINE   Interior surfaces highly polished—no tool marks.
              Chamber perfectly round, polished—no tool marks and concentric
                 with bore.
              Front sight properly seated, and centered—no protrusion into
                 barrel—square with receiver.
              Ribs straight and centered over bore—aligned with receiver—no
                 bumps or dips between stanchions.
              Magazine turning easily for taking gun apart and putting it together.

STOCK — Dense grain walnut—no sap wood. Good fit of stock to receiver
and   without appreciable excess of wood. Neatly fitted buttplate.
SLIDE HANDLE   Slide handle centered equi-distant from barrel walls.
              Lacquer finish lustrous, free from flaking, runs, or bubbles.

PATTERNS — Standard commercial loads in 30″ circle—40 yards

                     Full Choke—   approximately 67%
                     Modified Choke— approximately 50%
                     Imp. Cylinder— approximately 40%

              Center of pattern within 1″ of aiming point in any direction.

GENERAL — Action free from metal filings, chips, or foreign matter except light
                 grease for protection.
              Adequately wrapped and packed to prevent blemishing or damage
                 in shipment.

MODEL 50
AUTOLOADING SHOTGUN
ALL STYLES

WHAT OUR CUSTOMERS EXPECT

RECEIVER — Dulite blue-black finish over well polished exterior (Anodized on
and   Featherweight)
ACTION   Matting on receiver uniform, aligned with axis of bore and with rib
                 on ventilated rib barrels.
              Bolt face smooth, free from burrs, all cams burnished and polished.
              Guard closely fitted to receiver.
              Trigger lock positive but free from binding.
              Trigger adjusted to clean let-off at about 6 lbs.
              Action adjusted for positive feeding, extraction, and ejection for all
                 commercial loads.

BARREL — Dulite blue finish on well polished exterior surface-free from
                 circular thread-like marks.
              Interior surface smooth, highly polished, free of any impressions or
                 tool marks.
              Barrel lug solidly brazed to barrel.
              Front sight centered, properly seated, no protrusion into barrel.
              Ventilated ribs securely attached, straight and centered over axis of
                 bore. Ribs securely pinned against forward movement and tight
                 to stanchions.
              Barrel assembled and taken down with minimum effort.

STOCK and FOREARM — Of dense grain walnut—matching in grain and color. Lacquer, lustrous, free from flaking, runs or bubbles.

Checkering neatly done—clean, sharp, no run-off into borders; borders clean, no tearing, gouging or undulations. Patterns centered.

Close fit between grip of stock and receiver—very little overlapping of wood to metal and uniform around entire circumference.

Forearm has slight clearance, no side play when tightened.

Inside surface protected against moisture.

PATTERNS — Percentage of load in 30″ circle at 40 yards.

Full Choke— approximately 70%
Mod. Choke— approximately 50%
Imp. Cyl.— approximately 40%

Center of pattern within 1″ any direction from aiming point.

GENERAL — Action free of metal filings, chips, other foreign material except light grease for protection.

Careful wrapping and packing to prevent blemishing or damage in shipment.

TRAP AND SKEET

STOCK and FOREARM — Selected American Walnut, cap or pistol grip, butt plate or recoil pad neatly fitted. Stock and forearm well matched for color and grain.

Dimensions to be within ⅛″ as advertised on Skeet guns—1/16″ on Trap guns.

ACTION — Shell deflector on chamber.

PIGEON GRADE

STOCK and FOREARM — Full fancy American walnut, fancy checkering of finest workmanship. Careful fitting of stock to receiver, no excess of wood over metal. Buttplate or recoil pads carefully fitted. Stock and forearm well matched for grain and color. Pistol grip cap nicely fitted.

Pigeon engraved on receiver.
Hand smoothed working parts.
Bolt and carrier engine turned.

Appendix E
SHOTSHELL MISCELLANY

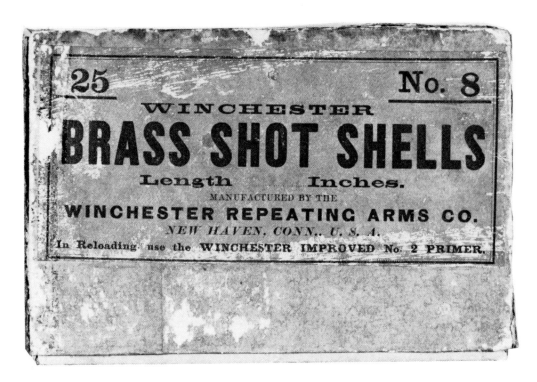

Nickel plated brass shotshells were offered beginning in 1882 for $2.50 more per 1000. The 8 gauge box above contained the nickeled cases and it is likely that the same label was used for them as for the standard unplated type in all gauges. The 8 gauge shells were made for single and double-barreled guns produced by other manufacturers. These side-labeled boxes are rarely seen, especially in 8 and 14 gauges.

25 WINCHESTER No. 12

BRASS SHOT SHELLS.

Length 2⅝ Inches.

MANUFACTURED BY THE

WINCHESTER REPEATING ARMS CO.

NEW HAVEN, CONN., U.S.A.

In Reloading, use the Winchester Improved No. 2 PRIMER.

25 No. 14

WINCHESTER

Brass Shot Shells.

Length 2⅝ Inches.

Manufactured by the

WINCHESTER REPEATING ARMS CO.,

NEW HAVEN, CONN., U.S.A.

In Reloading, use the Winchester Improved No. 2 Primer.

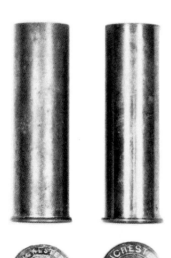

25 .58 Caliber.

WINCHESTER

BRASS SHOT SHELLS

Length Inches.

MANUFACTURED BY THE

WINCHESTER REPEATING

NEW HAVEN, CONN., U.S.A.

In Reloading, use the Winchester Improved No. 2 Copper Primer.

After the Civil War, a great many .58 cal. rifle-muskets came on the civilian market and many of them were converted to breech-loading shotguns. These shells were made for owners of those guns. Winchester did not make a .58 shotgun. Note the two sizes of headstamps.

179

Winchester sold empty and loaded 4 gauge shells for punt guns. Six are shown. From left above: (1) a first quality brass, (2) a purple paper shell (also made with tan and lime green paper), (3) a first quality black paper shell (also made with blue paper). From left below: (4) a green metal lined shell (also made in red), (5) a Winchester Leader and (6) a 1901 Leader. This fine specimen was once on a cartridge board. Some of these 1901 Leaders were factory loaded.

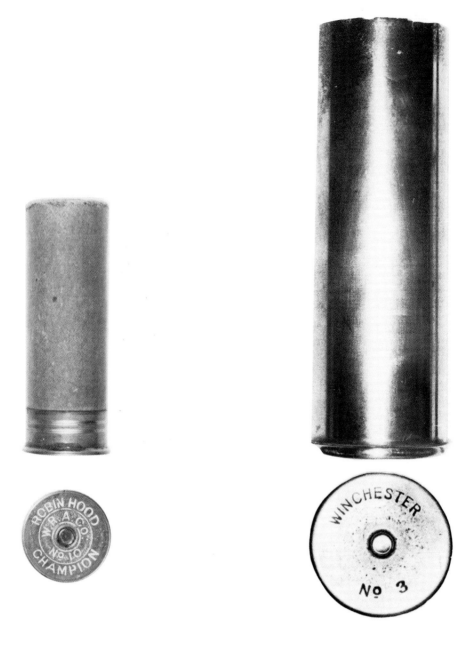

The base of the ROBIN HOOD CHAMPION 10 gauge shell has the double cannelure construction of the NUBLACK. Probably made prior to WWI, the reason for its manufacture remains obscure. Collectors doubt that Winchester would have made this shell for Robin Hood Ammunition Company, a competitor. (George Krienke collection)

The much-worn WINCHESTER NO. 3 was used in yacht cannons. (Bob McCarter collection, photos by Orin Reams)

BIBLIOGRAPHY

Barnes, Duncan, Watrous, George R., Rikhoff, James C., Hall, Thomas H., and Kuhlhoff, Pete, *The History of Winchester Firearms*, 1866–1980, Tulsa, Oklahoma, Winchester Press, 1980.

Bedlan, Felix A., "Winchester-Simmons Ventilated Ribs?" *The Winchester Collector*, June 1981 pp. 20–22.

Browning, John and Gentry, Curt, *John M. Browning American Gunmaker*, Garden City, New York, Doubleday and Company, 1964.

Kodl, Frank, "Letters," *Shootin Trap* vol. 3 no. 4 June 1981 p.10.

Madis, George, *The Winchester Book,* Brownsboro, Texas, Art and Reference House, 1977.

Madis, George, *The Winchester Handbook,* Brownsboro, Texas, Art and Reference House, 1981.

McIntosh, Michael, *The Best Shotguns Ever Made in America*, New York: Charles Scribner's Sons, 1981.

McIntosh, Michael, "The Winchester Model 21," *American Rifleman*, vol. 130, no. 2, February 1982, pp. 20–23 + .

McIntosh, Michael, "The Winchester Model 12," *American Rifleman*, vol. 129, no. 6, June 1981 pp. 30–33 + .

Simmons, Ernie Jr., typed response to questions March 1982.

Williamson, Harold F., *Winchester The Gun That Won The West*, New York: A. S. Barnes and Company, Inc., 1952.

Yearout, Lewis E., "The First Winchester Shotguns," *The Winchester Collector*, June, 1981 p.11.

INDEX

S

T

U

V

W

X

Y